T0325152

Finding What Matters Most to Patients

Finding What Matters Most to Patients

Forming the Foundation for Better Care

Thom Walsh, PhD

Routledge
Taylor & Francis Group

A PRODUCTIVITY PRESS BOOK

First edition published in 2019
By Routledge/Productivity Press
711 Third Avenue New York, NY 10017, USA
2 Park Square, Milton Park, Abingdon, Oxon OX14 4RN, UK

No claim to original U.S. Government works

Printed on acid-free paper

International Standard Book Number-13: 978-1-138-33987-3 (Hardback)

International Standard Book Number-13: 978-0-429-44086-1 (eBook)

*Routledge/Productivity Press is an imprint of Taylor & Francis Group, an
Informa business*

© 2019 by Thom Walsh, PhD

Library of Congress Cataloging-in-Publication Data

Names: Walsh, Thom, 1969- author.
Title: Finding what matters most to patients : forming the foundation for better care /
Thom Walsh, PhD.
Description: Boca Raton : Taylor & Francis, 2018. | Includes bibliographical references. |
Identifiers: LCCN 2018045718 (print) | LCCN 2018050694 (ebook) | ISBN 9780429440861 (e-Book)
| ISBN 9781138339873 (hardback : alk. paper)
Subjects: LCSH: Patient-centered health care. | Physician and patient. | Medical records. |
Communication in medicine.
Classification: LCC R727.3 (ebook) | LCC R727.3 .W339 2018 (print) | DDC 610.69/6–dc23
LC record available at https://lccn.loc.gov/2018045718

**Visit the Taylor & Francis Web site at
http://www.taylorandfrancis.com**

Ada N Walsh (1948–2017)
For Ada. Always.

Contents

Foreword

I met Thom Walsh in 1998 shortly after the innovative Dartmouth Spine Center opened its doors proclaiming "Back to work. Back to play. One back at a time." I remember talking with Dr. James Weinstein—the founder of the Spine Center (who went on to become Chair of Orthopedics, Director of the Dartmouth Institute and CEO of Dartmouth-Hitchcock Medical Center) when he told me about his latest "recruit." He said he had talked Thom Walsh, a rising star in physical therapy, to come to the Dartmouth Spine Center. Thom was a board-certified orthopedic clinical specialist and had done sub-specialty training at the McKenzie Institute in New Zealand, the international leader in the mechanical diagnosis and treatment of patients with pain and disability from spinal conditions. I started working with Thom shortly thereafter; we have been friends and colleagues since that time.

The Spine Center was a true innovation in delivering health care. It provided comprehensive and integrated care—one-stop shopping with wrap around services—by bringing together an interdisciplinary team ranging from doctors specializing in orthopedics, internal medicine, spinal surgery and pain management to physical therapy, psychology, and functional restoration. Not only was the mix of clinicians meant to match the diverse needs of spine patients, but the Spine Center also made the real-time use of PROMs (patient-reported outcome measures) in the flow of care and shared decision-making cornerstones of its program for delivering care, improving outcomes, and leading NIH-funded comparative effectiveness research on alternative treatment strategies.

Thom was a leading practitioner at the Spine Center for 8 years and then went on to earn his PhD at Dartmouth in Health Policy with a special emphasis on the clinical evaluative sciences, quality improvement, and health economics. In the next stage of his career, Thom focused on mainstreaming shared decision-making into diverse clinical programs at Dartmouth and became one of the most effective and popular professors in Dartmouth's graduate degree programs for MPH students and for mid-career physicians and administrators who came to Dartmouth to earn a masters degree in Heathcare Delivery Science from the Dartmouth Tuck School of Management and The Dartmouth Institute for Health Policy and Clinical Practice.

Thom's clinical experience and advanced education have combined to give him "double vision" by using his clinical vantage point as well as his academic lens. He sees how to make care more effective and more patient-centered from his extensive clinical experience as well as from a scholarly, evidence-based perspective. His special talent is to blend these two ways of knowing what works in the real world into something that is both easy to understand and practical to start applying in busy clinical settings.

Thom's new book reminds me of a current best seller in non-fiction titled *Astrophysics for People in a Hurry*. Both books deliver a lot of very important and fundamental information in a concise, easy-to-read package.

This book—*Finding What Matters Most to Patients*—tackles a key challenge for healthcare delivery. Despite the nation's enormous investment in paying for healthcare—approximately $28,000 per year for the average family of four people—and conducting research to discover new treatments and to restore health, we often fail to focus on the outcomes that matter most to patients.

The book's answer to this challenge (i.e., finding what matters most to patients and targeting care and treatments on improving the outcomes that in fact matter most) is to offer a three-point program.

1. **Patient-Reported Outcomes:** Use patient-reported information and PROMs to identify and assess the patient's needs as well as to track the patient's outcomes over time to determine their health benefit—i.e., how much they were helped in the ways that they wanted and needed to be helped.

2. **Shared Decision-Making:** Use shared decision-making (SDM) to match the patient's values and preferences with what biomedical science has to offer them based on best available evidence.

3. **Motivational Interviewing:** Use motivational interviewing (MI) to improve the conversations that patients have with clinicians to craft a personalized plan of care that the individual patient is ready, willing, and able to follow so as to realize the treatment benefit.

This three-point program is logical, practical, and doable. It's as easy as one, two, three: (1) use PROMs to find out what matters to patients, (2) use SDM to work to make the best treatment decisions taking into account evidence and patient preferences, and (3) use MI to help the patient to be capable and motivated to do what needs to be done. Back in time, when Thom was a physical therapist at the Dartmouth Spine Center, he began using and ultimately mastering all three of these techniques to become a highly regarded clinician who was known by his patients for his special manner and who was widely respected by his colleagues for his ability to help patients achieve optimal outcomes.

The saying "what matters most to patients" has become a popular phrase. It is hard to argue against taking this seriously if the aim is patient-centered care that helps people enjoy optimal health and well-being. What Thom Walsh does in this book is to start with the assumption that it is critical for clinicians to heed "what matters most to patients" and then to do something about it by using three specific methods to deliver patient-centered services. These methods can help clinicians to partner with their patients, to understand how they are doing healthwise using PROMs, the treatments most likely to improve their health using SDM, and how to work through the barriers to making the best treatment plan work for them in their everyday life using MI. The book provides a roadmap and guidance on how to develop the skill set needed to help patients to gain the benefits from healthcare that they value most highly. To sum up, this book "connects the dots" that can help patients get more health out of healthcare.

Biography

Dr. Nelson is a Professor of Community and Family Medicine at The Geisel School of Medicine at Dartmouth and The Dartmouth Institute for Health Policy and Clinical Practice. He serves as the Director of Population Health and Measurement at The Dartmouth Institute and leads a program on new models to advance the coproduction of healthcare. Dr. Nelson is a national leader in healthcare improvement and the development and application of measures of quality, system performance, health outcomes, value, and patient perceptions. Dr. Nelson's current work is focused on using patient-centered registries to become learning health systems capable of coproducing health, care, and science. He is currently leading a Dartmouth team that is conducting national proof-of-concept demonstration programs for several chronic disease popula-tions including cystic fibrosis, inflammatory bowel disease, and rheumatology.

In the early 1990s, Dr. Nelson and his colleagues at Dartmouth began developing clinical microsystem thinking. His work developing the "clinical value compass" and "whole system measures" to assess healthcare system performance has made him a well-recognized quality and value measurement expert.

He is the recipient of The Joint Commission's Ernest A. Codman award for his work on outcomes measurement in health care. Dr. Nelson has been a pioneer in bringing modern quality improvement thinking into the mainstream of health care; he helped launch the Institute for Healthcare Improvement and served as a founding Board Member. He has authored over 150 publications and is an author of two recent books:

1. *Quality by Design: A Clinical Microsystems Approach*
2. *Value by Design: Developing Clinical Microsystems to Achieve Organizational Excellence.*

He received an AB from Dartmouth College, an MPH from Yale University, and a DSc from Harvard University.

Eugene C. Nelson

Foreword

A key distinction between industrial health care and patient care is what role the patient ought to play in the production of value. Industrial health care, at its worst, places the patient as an employee on the factory floor. The system expects patients to act responsibly and execute any tasks and medical errands assigned to them. To this end, the system should "empower" and "activate" patients to improve their productivity. A similar set of expectations is placed on the other employee there—clinicians. These professionals must "deliver care" according to standards and document it properly to obtain full credit for the work. Payers and their surrogates then determine if the work produced by these employees is worthy of reimbursement. Through this lens, industrial processes should optimize the production of better population outcomes at lower costs.

This system is capable of near-miracle moments of technical excellence. Patients report moments—accidents, really—of deep human connection and care. This industrial health care system, however, consumes increasingly greater resources, routinely produces poor patient outcomes, and results in care provider burnout. About forty percent of patients report being unable to do all that is expected of them. Worse still, those unable to fulfill these expectations, or simply swamped by them, are labeled as "noncompliant." Meanwhile, across the desk, a record number of clinicians report symptoms of depersonalization and loss of empathy, the hallmarks of burnout. Suicide, divorce, and leaving the practice of medicine are some of its consequences.

Patient care can seem impossible in a system in which the means applied to achieve caring—such as money—has become the end for which care is merely a means. Healthcare companies invest heavily in clinical activities that are better reimbursed, finding more "mission" where the money is, rather than deploying resources to advance their true mission. In this way, the offer of care in mental health or rehabilitation, and of social support, is often insufficient, while cardiovascular, cancer, ophthalmological, and orthopedic care is oversupplied. Driven by this corrupted form of "no money, no mission," marketing entices patients to consume health care and optimize the companies' income while payers place barriers to drive down consumption and expenditures. In this scenario, patients-turned-consumers are expected to shop around and consider that "less is more" as they "choose wisely." Patients get seduced by the promise of innovations and services and become frustrated by payer denials and unexpectedly onerous bills.

There is an alternative to industrial health care. This alternative requires that clinicians see patients in high definition. This means being able to appreciate his or her problematic situation with clarity, identifying with each patient the aspect of that situation that requires action. It requires patients and care providers to work together in conversation, to uncover alternatives that may bring resolution to the problem and to consider "trying them on for size" until the best way forward becomes clear. Collaborative approaches, including shared decision-making and motivational interviewing, benefit from such a clear view of the patient situation and rely on profoundly human forms of communication to invent a way forward. This alternative protects the space and time in which these interactions can take place and renders them with minimal friction or interruption, without waste, but also without haste. In these unhurried consultations, clinicians can appreciate the humanity of the other, the privilege of the bedside they enjoy, and the potential to care—not to "deliver" or "provide" care, but to care. It is in these moments that patients and clinicians connect and make meaning together. For patients, this helps form a therapeutic alliance with their clinicians. For clinicians, this fuels their vocation and renews their commitment to serve. And this is what matters most.

In *Finding What Watters Most to Patients*, Dr. Walsh describes how to begin implementing this alternative approach to industrialized medicine. Here, we determine how well we provide care by noticing how well patients say we are doing to ensure that care is not only scientific and capable of optimal outcomes, but that it also makes sense to each patient. In this way, there is no need to turn patients and caregivers into unpaid employees. Rather, we can respect their precious time, energy, and attention, and, instead of overwhelming them with tasks, leave as much time as possible to pursue patients' hopes and dreams. Focusing on what matters most as Thom has outlined is an antidote to industrial health care and a hallmark of careful and kind care.

Biography

Victor M. Montori, MD, is a Professor of Medicine at Mayo Clinic, an endocrinologist, and a health services researcher. Dr. Montori is the author of more than 600 peer-reviewed publications. His productivity during the last decade places him among the top one percent of cited researchers within clinical medicine worldwide. He is a Senior Advisor at the Center for Evidence and Practice Improvement in the Agency for Healthcare Quality and Research in the United States. He also serves on the Editorial Advisory Board of *TheBMJ*, and as Director of Late-Stage Translational Research at the Mayo Center for Clinical and Translational Science. He is a recognized expert in evidence-based medicine and shared decision-making, and a developer of the concept of minimally disruptive medicine. He works in Rochester, Minnesota, at Mayo Clinic's KER Unit, to advance person-centered care for patients with diabetes and other chronic conditions. He recently published the book *Why We Revolt: A Patient Revolution for Careful and Kind Care.*

Victor M. Montori

Acknowledgments

Nine professionals whose interviews make up the last chapter of this book and whom I had never met, created space in their busy lives to respond to my emails and talk with me. I am thankful for their time and inspired by the work they do. I trust you will be too.

Lee Reeder is my editor and has become a friend. My writing and life are better for it.

I am thankful for the assistance from Katherine Kadian and Kristine Mednansky from Taylor & Francis.

Several colleagues, including Tim Link, Matt Grimes, Meghan Longacre, and Jeff Alderman regularly inform and refine my thoughts on the science of healthcare delivery. I try to thank them regularly, but it is not enough. They help more than they know.

My students and clients push me to be more clear and practical. They, too, have contributed to my work more than they know.

I believe it is important to acknowledge, you, the reader. You have chosen to read books like this out of a desire to improve the delivery of healthcare. That is a noble cause. Improvement efforts are always in addition to caring for patients and administrative duties. They are considered by many to be extra and best avoided. These extra efforts are often more difficult than imagined, take longer than planned, and usually involve at least one crisis along the way.

Furthermore, it is possible to go days or even weeks without anyone saying thank you in appreciation for the extra burden you volunteer to bear. I want you to know that I appreciate you.

Author

Thom Walsh, PhD, is the Founder and Chief Strategy Officer of Cardinal Point Healthcare Solutions, an Adjunct Lecturer at the Dartmouth Institute for Health Policy and Clinical Practice, and a Visiting Associate Professor of Community Medicine at the Oxley College of Health Sciences at the University of Tulsa. He holds an MS degree in Physical Therapy, an MS in Clinical Evaluative Sciences, and a PhD in Health Policy. Known as an excellent teacher and mentor, he draws on extensive clinical, research, and consulting experience to help people and organizations to navigate a rapidly changing healthcare environment. His clinical career spanned private practice and academic settings, including the development and launch of a multidisciplinary spine center at the Dartmouth-Hitchcock Medical Center. His writings on patient-reported outcome measures, healthcare costs and utilization, shared decision-making, motivational interviewing, and ethical leadership have appeared in numerous publications, including the *BMJ, JAMA, Spine, The Journal of Healthcare Management, Forbes, The New America Foundation*, and *The Atlantic*. His first book, *Navigating to Value in Healthcare*, was released in 2017. Dr. Walsh also enjoys hiking, running, reading, and writing. He volunteers with a mountain search and rescue unit and Team Rubicon, a disaster relief and humanitarian aid organization.

Chapter 1

The long road to finding what matters most to patients

Healthcare leaders are dealing with greater chaos and uncertainty. When it comes to the information they need to assess where they are and where they are going, they need help. The essential data such leaders need on the value of the services is often lacking or missing, because they are not adequately collecting and using data on outcomes that matter to patients or on the costs associated with achieving those outcomes. Despite the apparent recognition of the importance of patient-reported outcomes, few organizations have started to develop the capacity to measure them, to understand the costs of producing the care they deliver, and to govern change.

In March 2017, researchers examined the attitudes of healthcare executives, clinical leaders, and clinicians about what data are most important now in health care and how they anticipate that will change in the future. The findings, published in the *NEJM Catalyst* and titled "Care Redesign: What Data Can Really Do for Health Care," indicated that currently clinical data are rated the highest by far, at 92%, while ranked second and third were, respectively, cost data (56%) and claims data (45%). However, when asked about what they believed would be the most valuable data sources in five years, the participants anticipated that claims data would drop off significantly (scoring only 32%), and clinical and cost data would be joined at the top by patient-generated data and genomic data (both scoring 40%).

Participants in this study were also asked to select what they believed to be the biggest opportunities for the use of data in health care, and 81% of them put care coordination at the top of the list, followed closely by improved decision support for patients and providers at 79%.

These results point to the rapidly growing importance of patient-reported outcomes, measures of care coordination, and improved decision support. These areas need to be prioritized if we are to truly navigate toward greater value in healthcare. These data form the foundation for providing better care to each patient, along with greater collaboration between patients and providers, and greater coordination between teams of providers. However, in order to take advantage of the promise of patient-reported data, we have to know how to use it to our best advantage.

Building a sustainable healthcare system will be more difficult and take longer than previously promised because the system we have now is profitable for many of us. However, it is not financially sustainable over the long run—not for patients, not our communities, nor the healthcare system as a whole.

For the necessary changes to happen, we need to create systems and processes that reliably produce high-quality outcomes that matter to patients, keep costs under control, accurately identify patient preferences, and coordinate care to meet patients' needs. If we build a healthcare system like this, it will be sustainable regardless of political winds and the latest acronyms, because it will be able to document the value of the care it is providing to its patient population.

A healthcare system that can demonstrably improve outcomes, align the care its patients receive with each patient's informed preferences, and coordinate its care in a manner that is observable by patients while keeping costs contained is delivering high-value care. Care delivered in this manner is good business, regardless of the latest reimbursement schemes. While good value is good business, it is not easy to create a delivery system that is agile enough to act on the data collected. There will be resistance. In my experience, the resistance to those changes can be overcome when we create an environment that emphasizes learning more about—and from—those measurements.

So you might ask, "Why do I want to know what matters most to patients?" Without a thought, many reflexively respond that the justification for developing any major program in our current healthcare climate is "the business case."

1.1 The siren call of the business case

Every year my clients and students raise concerns about how much time it might take to add components of patient-reported outcome measures (PROMs), shared decision-making, and motivational interviewing to office visits, which I will explore in detail in this book. Discussions about time are really talks about money, where the concern is that spending more time with a patient will decrease the time available for seeing more patients, which makes a provider less efficient.

In a volume-based reimbursement model, longer visits lead to lower volume and decreased revenue. Early attempts at improving the adoption of shared decision-making and motivational interviewing consisted of promoting their effectiveness. Patients changed their minds when they were fully informed of their treatment options and aware of their preferences. Higher rates of successful behavior change were found when patients reported improved motivation, more confidence, and less ambivalence. The "effectiveness push" did help with the dissemination of the concepts of shared decision-making and motivational interviewing, but it did little to improve the adoption of the techniques because it did nothing to address the potentially lost revenue.

During the past decade, as reimbursement models began to shift from volume to value, advocates have adopted another approach to improve the adoption of shared decision-making and motivational interviewing. For simplicity's sake, this approach can be labeled "the business case." The foundation for the business case rests on several studies that found patients tended to be more risk-averse after learning about their treatment options. Patients fully informed of the treatment options tended to choose invasive treatments less often than patients who had not participated in a shared decision-making protocol. Fewer invasive procedures would mean less expensive care, which led to savings in a value-based model.

It is possible to make a similar business case for motivational interviewing in the era of value-based care. Patients with a high degree of ambivalence and low confidence required more visits to manage their chronic conditions. Motivational interviewing works to decrease ambivalence and increase confidence, thus improving the likelihood of successful behavioral changes that are required to better manage their condition. Fewer office visits meant lost revenue in volume-based models but could lead to savings in value-based settings.

Researchers and advocates took the results found in these studies and extrapolated to the wider population. For example, using numbers selected for easy math, if a knee replacement costs $10,000 and 40% of a study sample of 100 patients decline the procedure after participating in a shared decision-making protocol, this yields a savings of $400,000 (40 patients × $10,000 saved for each). Extrapolating to a population of one million patients with arthritis of the knee produces a "savings" of four billion dollars (400,000 patients × $10,000 saved for each). Applied across multiple conditions and using similar calculations for motivational interviewing, the potential "savings" soon reached tens of billions of dollars per year, thus making an apparently strong business case for wider dissemination and adoption of the techniques.

1.1.1 The faulty logic of the business case

As you may have already concluded, there are problems with these types of calculations. First, the universe of diagnoses studied is relatively small compared to all possible diagnoses, and while many of the studies found reduced utilization of services and procedures, not all did. Even in the small number of studies, some patients chose surgery more often, not less, after participating in a shared decision-making protocol. It is impossible to know whether more studies done with more patients and conditions would always find lower utilization of services.

Second, the studies conducted so far have not been particularly rigorous and have been prone to bias. For example, the costs associated with performing shared decision-making and motivational interviewing are difficult to measure and seldom included in these forecasts. In addition, the studies used relatively short time horizons, which might have missed downstream costs. For example, a patient deemed eligible for a spinal fusion procedure who initially declines the operation today, after learning of the risks and benefits of additional options, would appear to produce a savings if our time horizon is one year. However, five years later, she might return to the decision-making process and choose surgery after experiencing worsening symptoms. In this type of case, the procedure is delayed, not forgone, and in either circumstance, additional therapies and treatments were not typically included in the cost model.

Combined, these circumstances raise concerns of overpromising the savings, which may have a paradoxical effect of decreasing the adoption of shared decision-making and motivational interviewing. If a potential savings of $10 billion motivates wider dissemination of these techniques but only $4 billion is achieved, should we stop informing patients of their options? What if adopting the communication techniques ultimately costs $1 billion? Do we reverse course then?

The problem is that reliance on a business case to motivate improved communication between healthcare providers and patients makes us shallow and inhumane and pits financial concerns against ethical behavior. Research has shown that patients change their minds when they learn more about the treatment choices available to them. As an active part of the treatment team, patients help achieve congruence between what matters most and the care received. That alone is a good thing, and we should work to adopt techniques that increase the likelihood of congruence regardless of the reimbursement model.

This is not to say that economic considerations are irrelevant. Indeed, several cost allocation principles can help us optimize the adoption of effective communication techniques and can be applied in volume- or value-based reimbursement settings.

As clinical leaders and providers, when we seek to add value in health care, we accomplish it by looking for ways to improve the patient's outcomes and experience with the care process. The goal is to remove non-value-added steps and redesign variations that add costs or do not improve outcomes.

When it comes to health care, patients do not generally care so much about mortality rate statistics and clinical quality indicators—they care about how a treatment will affect their well-being and ability to continue to actively participate in life and society. Because of this, there is often a gulf between what matters most to patients and what providers believe matters to them. Plainly put, care providers are not very accurate judges of what patients will choose when they are empowered with information and options and can relate them to how they want to live their lives.

For example, more than two-thirds of oncologists believe "saving my breast" would be a high-priority outcome for their breast cancer patients, while less than a fifth of their patients actually feel that is a high-priority outcome for them. When orthopedic surgeons were asked to examine a cohort of patients with osteoarthritis of the knee to determine those who would be most likely to prefer knee replacement surgery, they were dead wrong, with only about 15% of those eligible choosing to proceed.

Employing PROMs and using techniques such as shared decision-making and motivational interviewing help to avoid a misdiagnosis—a word that you will find takes on new and multiple meanings in the new environment I present in this book. Moreover, employing these measures and techniques offers several additional benefits for healthcare providers. Here are just a few:

■ As a provider, you will gain more satisfaction because better informed patients are better able to collaborate with the healthcare team to make the "correct" treatment and management decisions for themselves.
■ When you give patients evidence-based information, you save time over having to clarify the confusion created when they do their own research through the Internet or word of mouth.
■ Patients who are highly involved in their course of treatment are less likely to sue.
■ In employing shared decision-making and motivational interviewing, you are overcoming ambivalence, which is the first step toward changing behavior for the better.

1.2 A history of outcomes measurement

The routine collection of medical outcomes and their use in health care have a long history, going back more than 150 years; however, efforts to measure patient-reported outcomes has only been a focus for the past 30 years. Resistance to the use of both medical and patient-reported outcomes has been strong and the march toward their widespread acceptance and application has been slow, with most of the progress occurring only in the past several decades.

It is generally accepted that in the 1850s, during the Crimean War, nursing pioneer and social reformer Florence Nightingale was the first healthcare professional to systematically collect data for the purposes of improving care outcomes. Noting that wounded soldiers died more frequently from complications of the care they received than from their initial injuries, she began tracking vital signs and care processes. Her aim was to try to determine causes of increased mortality among certain soldiers compared to others. To that end, she adopted an innovative approach. Rather than focusing on mortality as the only outcome that mattered, she flipped the frame and examined what factors were associated with the restoration of health. She classified her patients as relieved, unrelieved, or dead. During the course of this work, she found significant correlations between sanitation conditions and infections, long before germ theory was well understood. She was able to increase a soldier's chance of survival by emphasizing cleanliness and routine practices for the observation and care of her patients. Despite the success of her methods, they were not widely adopted until much later. Indeed, struggles to achieve adequate hand washing by healthcare providers remain to this very day.

In the early 20th century, Boston physician E. A. Codman collected data to improve the delivery of health care. He tracked patients with what he called "end-result cards." These five-by-eight-inch pieces of paper he kept on each patient included basic demographic data, along with information on diagnosis, treatment, and the case's outcome. Codman followed up with each patient for at least one year. He believed that through such an "end-results system," he could identify medical errors and unintended side effects, improve care processes and decrease mortality rates.

While Codman is now widely regarded as the father of outcomes management in patient care, in his own time, his work was derided. Codman believed in transparency. He believed end-result cards would transform care if used by all physicians, for all patients, and the findings were publicly reported, including any specifics on medical errors. He believed the public would use this information to guide their choices for hospitals and care types. His ideas were too innovative for the medical community of his time, and his peers ostracized him.

It was not until much later in the 20th century that physician Avedis Donabedian created a ground-breaking framework that pushed medical outcomes to the forefront in evaluating the quality of health care. Although there have been several noteworthy frameworks for evaluating health-care quality over the years, the Donabedian model is still considered the standard, because he realized that Codman's end results were dependent on factors Codman had not considered. Donabedian described how the relationship between the structure of care systems and the process of care delivery influenced medical outcomes. He noted that the best way to design care systems and clinical processes was by identifying best outcomes and reverse-engineering what had occurred.

Using the Donabedian model, the information used to evaluate health care comes from the following categories: structure, process, and outcomes. These categories are briefly outlined below:

■ *Structure* refers to the care setting, including facilities, equipment, program operations, administrative structures, the qualifications of providers and staff, administration structure, and operations of programs. In recent years, this has expanded to include healthcare information technology.

■ *Process* refers to the provision of care and whether it is appropriate, complete, acceptable, and provided competently. More recently, Harvard researchers have advocated process mapping as a central feature of time-driven, activity-based costing method for calculating the cost of delivering care.

■ *Outcomes* refer to the end results of care—the effects of health care on patients or larger populations. These can include recovery, survival, and changes in health status. Less concrete outcomes can include patient satisfaction, increased patient knowledge of their conditions and options, and attitudes about their quality of life as it relates to health. Until recently, healthcare providers selected the outcomes that were assessed. This included even patient satisfaction, and health status measures where the list of measures selected originated from a long list of possible measures generated through a process of professional consensus.

As the Donabedian model for evaluating and improving the delivery of healthcare has proliferated throughout the industry and a greater proportion of patients were surviving for longer periods, the need for outcomes to evolve became evident. For example, in both Nightingale's and Codman's eras, twin brothers with the same disease and cared for by the same doctors at the same facility would both be satisfied to be alive if the only outcome assessed was measured as dead or alive immediately after their treatment. Today, more people are living for years with chronic conditions and treatment options have increased substantially. Those same twin brothers, say one a concert pianist and the other a piano mover, if treated today, might have very different preferences about their treatments and might also prioritize different aspects of their health.

1.3 Patient-reported outcomes evolve

Healthcare outcome pioneers Nightingale, Codman, and Donabedian all based their observations on clinical outcomes such as death, X-ray results, blood tests, and expert opinion. While it can be argued that some of these measures were patient-centered, none were patient-reported, nor did the idea to measure them originate from patients.

True PROMs have only come into common use during the past 30 years, beginning in research trials. Today, researchers continue to collect these measures, base sample size calculations on them, and generate hypotheses based on expected changes in the measures. All of this often happens with little or no involvement by care providers.

Next, learning collaboratives began sharing de-identified and aggregated PROMs to better understand the linkage between processes and outcomes across their networks, and in registries they may participate in, including The National Spine Network or the American Joint Replacement Registry (JRR), which was originally the California JRR. Although registries provide aggregated data for process improvement, it is still uncommon for a practice or organization to have robust systems and processes in place to disseminate findings, implement tests of change, assess the impact of the change, and share findings across departmentalized service lines.

More recently, many providers have been exposed to PROMs through the Physician Quality Reporting System (PQRS) and payment reform legislation such as the Medicare Access and CHIP Reauthorization Act (MACRA) and its Merit-based Incentive Payment System (MIPS), which employs

PROMs. Within payment models such as the Hospital Value-Based Purchasing Program and MACRA/MIPS, healthcare services may reward or punish healthcare providers based on aggregated PROMs, providing a bottom-line business case for practices and hospitals to employ PROMs.

The patient-reported outcomes seen in research and registries and for reimbursement share a couple of important features. They are first aggregated and then reported to providers as a range of values with mean or median values, and there is a lag between the collection of the data and the report to providers. The lag is often substantial. The comparison of a range of values for one group to that of another is an effective way to assess the degree of variation between the comparators; further, comparing mean or median values between two groups is useful for to evaluate treatment effects. It is, however, difficult to perform such analyses and glean important clinical information from them when there is a lag between an action and feedback regarding the effects of the action.

Aggregated PROMs, and the lag that occurs in reporting them, are limited in their ability to inform the care of an individual patient at the point of care, and they are consequently limited in their ability to influence provider behavior. Today's technology can allow patients to securely complete surveys using their cell phones. Apps, cloud-based data storage, big data analytics, and data visualization tools make it relatively easy for the data a patient enters to be immediately available for the treatment provider to review during an appointment. Using the same technology, the patient's data can be compared with group and/or population norms in order to give providers more context.

An individual patient's reported measures can inform the communication between the patient and the provider, helping both to identify and discuss what matters most to the patient. The provider can then respond immediately and take care to align treatment plans with the patient's priorities. This helps to speed up the process of identifying what matters most to the patient and helps to ensure the treatment plan addresses those concerns. When used over time, these data help to focus discussions around what matters most and whether the treatment plan is working as expected, or not.

Around this point, some clinicians will push back on using PROMs. Their resistance usually begins with a statement that goes something like this: "I already know all of this from talking with my patients." I first respond by agreeing that a proper history done by a thoughtful provider can identify the patient's complaints and what matters most to the patient about those complaints. It is not always easy, but I have seen it done many times. In fact, I would go so far as to say that the vast majority of providers can be this communicative on their best days. The problem, I propose, is that "best days" are infrequent. Instead, we are tired, rushed, and frustrated too often. We are also complex humans with nonclinical events that affect our day involving our families, friends, and communities. Given that we are not always at our best, wouldn't it be nice to have better, quicker, and more reliable insight into our patients' perceptions of their overall health, their physical well-being, and their mental health? Much like an MRI of a patient's lumbar spine provides insight into the potential anatomic explanation for a patient's pain and loss of function, PROMs provide insight into how the patient copes with the pain and is adjusting to or accommodating the loss of function.

There is a difference between the anatomic explanations for a patient's symptoms and how the patient is able to fare with the symptoms. Providers will frequently claim, "Of course there is a difference between anatomic or physiologic findings and symptoms." Nevertheless, most providers are surprised by the degree of discordance when they start using PROMs at the point of service. It is a learning process and takes time to understand that successfully medicating, repairing, or replacing the anatomic or physiologic finding may or may not change the patient's perception of their health, their sense of physical well-being, or their mental well-being.

The purpose of this book is to help providers to better understand how to use PROMs to their advantage at the point of service. To do so, I will provide background information to develop some shared knowledge and shared language. I will also provide examples of a provider's dialogue with a patient using PROMs at several points in an episode of care. In addition, I have interviewed several providers who have significant experience using PROMs. In those interviews, I asked how they started, what they have learned, what problems they experienced, the solutions they found, and what advice they would offer for someone just beginning to use PROMs.

Introducing the observe—orient—decide—act (OODA) loop up front in the book is important in giving insight into why it is vital for us to expend a good amount of effort in avoiding a misdiagnosis. I believe that the OODA loop, borrowed from air-to-air-combat decision-making, is highly relevant to the value-based healthcare environment of today. Healthcare providers and patients can work together to observe the available information from many variables, orient themselves to their current situation and resources, decide on the best course of action based on patient preferences and informed choices, and come together to the point of acting on that decision. The goal, and often the result, of this process is a solution based on what matters most to the patient.

From the introduction of the OODA loop, I will present patient-reported outcome models in order to instill an appreciation for the disconnect that often occurs between provider-centric measures and the things that really matter to individual patients. Patient-centric care takes into account the experiences, perspectives, needs, and preferences of patients. PROMs redefine what is meant by the "best" outcome for the patient and create the necessity for a higher level of involvement from the patient in the treatment and management of their conditions. Patient-reported outcome tools increase patient involvement by allowing them to report their perceptions of their health and what they consider to be good outcomes from care and treatment.

After introducing these models, I will explore how PROMs can be used at the point of service—the provider–patient interaction. I present examples of one-on-one discussions designed to encourage the kinds of interactions that create a collaborative environment. This will set the stage for more in-depth insight into tools for optimizing the use of PROs, including shared decision-making and motivational interviewing that I present later.

In introducing models of shared decision-making, I stress the value of balancing risks with patient preferences and values, which is a cornerstone of the definition of shared decision-making. We will learn that getting to that balance is a little more complex than some might imagine. The detailed look at the 3-Talk Model of engaging patients in discussions about their treatment choices will explain the process of getting to the ultimate goal of making a shared decision, a collaborative discussion of available options between a thoughtful provider and an informed patient.

From there, we will delve more deeply into the discussion between provider and patient through the concept of motivational interviewing—a package of techniques and processes designed to overcome the major barrier to positive behavior change, which is ambivalence. We will show examples of how motivational interviewing techniques and their processes can help patients get past their ambivalence and gain the confidence that can help them drive positive changes in their health.

Bibliography

Compton-Phillips, A. (2017, March). Care redesign: What data can really do for health care (insights report). *NEJM Catalyst*. http://catalyst.nejm.org/effectiveness-healthcare-data-survey-analysis/.

Donabedian, A. (2003). *An introduction to quality assurance in health care.*1st ed. Vol. 1. New York: Oxford University Press.

Neuhauser, D. (2002). Heroes and martyrs of quality and safety: E. A.Codman. *Quality and Safety in Health Care*11, no. 1:104–105.https://www.ncbi.nlm.nih.gov/pmc/articles/PMC1743579/pdf/v011p00104.pdf.

Nightingale, F. (1863/1986). *Notes on hospitals.* 1st ed. London, West Strand: John W. Parker and Son. https://archive.org/details/notesonhospital01nighgoog.

Chapter 2

Introducing the OODA loop

Before we proceed to detailing patient-reported outcome measures and methods for collecting and optimizing their use, we need to address why it is important for us to make this effort. We also need to look at our definitions of value from both the provider's and the patient's perspectives.

A misdiagnosis can be a nightmare. Patients worry they could receive treatment that is not indicated. This worry is second only to the concern that a curative treatment is possible but the treatable condition is left unidentified. Care providers have bad dreams about a misdiagnosis, too. A misdiagnosis leads to unnecessary tests or treatments, thus exposing patients to potential harms with no possibility for benefit or delaying needed care. Payers for health care worry about the costs associated with tests and treatments that are not appropriately targeted, and society worries that the costs of care are consuming funds that could be better spent on public goods that can improve the well-being of populations, such as education and infrastructure.

While medical misdiagnosis is what typically comes to mind when one hears of the word *misdiagnosis*, that is not the only type of misdiagnosis. A preference misdiagnosis occurs when a patient receives a test or treatment that he/she would not have chosen, had he/she been fully informed of his/her available options. A readiness misdiagnosis occurs when a patient receives a treatment advice requiring actions from the patient that he/she is ambivalent about, lacks confidence in, or lacks the necessary resources to complete.

Patients, providers, and payers consider only the medical misdiagnosis when thinking about health care, but all three types of misdiagnosis contribute to ineffective and inefficient care. Fully informed patients, once cognizant of their preferences, often choose less invasive or less involved care than do more naïve patients. Patients who are emotionally ready to take actions meant to improve their health and who are confident in their ability to complete the action are more likely to become self-sufficient more quickly.

Care providers could suffer financially as a result of a misdiagnosis regardless of payment mechanism. The financial incentives reward a correct diagnosis and punish a misdiagnosis. However, in a volume-based payment system, the incentives are perverse for preference and readiness diagnoses. A misdiagnosis of either leads to more tests and treatments, and consequently larger payments in volume-based payment models.

In value-based payment models, incentives are aligned for all three types of misdiagnosis. Providers are rewarded when they can get the medical diagnosis correct, recognize when an informed patient prefers a less expensive treatment, and align treatment recommendations with a patient's readiness to perform any actions that may be required of him/her.

The trend toward value-based payment systems means care providers must become more aware their patients' preferences and readiness. An approach is needed that helps providers to observe what matters most to their patients about their medical diagnosis, their preferences, and their readiness. After observing, care providers need to orient, or bring to bear, the tests and treatments that best address each patient's medical needs. Often, multiple options are available and a collaborative approach is needed to decide which choice is best aligned with the patient's preferences. After deciding, action is required. In many instances, the patient is not a passive recipient of a treatment; rather, his active participation is required for an optimal outcome. Financial rewards go to providers who observe, orient, decide, and act effectively and efficiently in value-based payment systems. Over time, new actions produce new outcomes, treatments are reoriented, decisions are revisited, and new actions are taken, creating an observe–orient–decide–act, or OODA loop.

2.1 OODA loop background

The OODA loop may be unfamiliar to healthcare professionals, but it is not new. John Boyd, a retired and now deceased Air Force colonel, first described the components of OODA loop in 1976 as a conceptual model for training pilots in air-to-air combat. According to Boyd, when pilots faced off in a dogfight, the ultimate victor would be the one who was able to observe the necessary information from a broad stream of variables, orient the aircraft and additional resources to the best possible position, decide on the most advantageous course of action, and rapidly act on that decision.

Boyd found the conceptual model necessary because he understood humans will resort to mental models to rapidly understand and adapt in changing environments, and in a world of limited resources and skills, decisions and actions become critical determinants of survival. Our biggest liability is our inability to appropriately and rapidly recognize our emerging circumstances. Instead, we usually fail to shift our perspective soon enough because we exert great effort in our attempts to fit the new information into existing models, or our sense of how the world "should be."

Excellent observation and orientation help differentiate the key variables and to deduce the most important immediate decision from among many possible decision points over time. The resulting knowledge then motivates the next action. However, it is not enough to break down a situation into isolated domains. If left at this point, any knowledge gained would only result in stove-piped chaos. The particular effect resulting from the selected action must then be resynthesized into a more complete picture in order to maintain situational awareness. In this manner, the OODA loop represents a cycle of differential deduction and reintegration.

A fighter pilot relies on a dizzying array of instrument panels that relay an enormous amount of data. The data are arranged so that the most important information can be seen and understood at a glance. The data are real-time and serve to feed-forward information to the pilot to immediately influence subsequent actions. In addition to current performance, the data are norm-based and provide pilots with immediate feedback if their performance deviates from the norm. In addition, data from a flight are saved and reviewed later to help a pilot learn more rapidly than he/she might otherwise. Aggregated data can create simulations, so that all pilots in the squadron can gain experience more rapidly.

2.2 The OODA loop applied to patient care

The OODA loop concept, combined with the use of patient-reported outcomes at the point of care, shared decision-making, and motivational interviewing, can help care providers adapt to the trend toward value-based payment systems by gaining more awareness of what matters most to their patients, along with their patients' preferences and readiness to act.

The starting point is **observation** of what matters to a patient via the use of patient-reported measures. While easy

enough in the abstract, there are leadership challenges associated with the changes in strategy, operations, and culture
that are required to put the needed systems and processes into
place. However, once the measures are in place, observation
of what matters becomes relatively easy, like reading a lab
report or reviewing an MRI.

Following observation, the patient and care provider can
jointly **orient** themselves to where they are currently and
what courses of action are available. With multiple options
available, the shared decision-making process helps the
patient and care provider to efficiently **decide** on the care
path that is most aligned with what matters most to the patient
and his/her informed preferences. The patient and care
provider may decide to **act** on a plan only to then realize
executing the plan requires more commitment than anticipated. Patients can lack confidence and/or feel ambivalent
about their ability to successfully complete the required
actions, even though the idea of the action aligns with their
preferences.

In the next chapter, we will begin learning more about the
different types of patient-reported measures, the strengths and
weaknesses of each type, and their construction. In addition,
we will examine the provider language that helps to integrate the new measures more smoothly and to glean greater
insight into what matters most to patients during an initial
visit with a patient.

Bibliography

Miller, W. R. and S. Rollnick. (2002). *Motivational interviewing:
Preparing people to change*. 2nd ed. New York: The Guilford
Press.
Rollnick, S., W. R.Miller, and C. C. Butler. (2008). *Motivational inter-
viewing in health care: Helping patients change behavior*. New
York: The Guilford Press.

Chapter 3

Patient-reported measures help find what matters most

Throughout much of the history of quality improvement in patient care, efforts to improve care focused narrowly on the process, tracking whether care providers followed particular standards or "best practices" during the course of care to increase the likelihood of desired outcomes. In these early days, true outcome measures were infrequent, but where they existed, care providers selected them. Measures such as blood pressure for patients with hypertension, A1C levels for patients with diabetes, and imaging results following joint replacement or spinal surgery were commonly monitored outcomes because they were relatively easy to define and had anatomic or physiologic relevance for the provider. Patients, however, did not come to the care provider because their A1C level was high or their hip joint showed signs of degeneration. Patients sought care because of pain and/or a worrisome change in their ability to perform activities that matter to them.

Recognition of the disconnect between care provider–centric measures and what mattered most to patients led the move toward patient-centered care, in which care is built around the experiences, perspectives, needs, and preferences of patients. The addition of patient-centric measures does not negate, supplant, or make less relevant the anatomic and physiologic measures that care providers are most accustomed to. Rather, the patient-centric measures are additional information that can help care providers more quickly identify what matters to individual patients and triage their care decisions. Patient involvement in the creation process has driven the evolution of the patient-centric measures. More recently, psychometricians have begun interviewing patients and using focus groups of patients to identify concepts that matter to them in order to then create surveys that assess the identified concepts. Surveys created in this way are not only patient-centered and patient-reported—the survey items themselves are patient-generated.

3.1 Patient-centered outcome measurement

In general terms, patient-centered care is care organized around the patient. In the early development of patient-centered models of care, outcome measures still reported on outcomes that health care providers believed were best for their patients, based on evidence from a variety of sources. Patient-centered research focused on collecting and analyzing outcome measures used mainly to inform a patient's consent with options for their treatment and care management. To collect this information, researchers relied mostly on available provider-centric data sources, disease registries, electronic health record (EHR) data, administrative claims information, and aggregated results from prior research. This information determined the treatment and care management alternatives that would most likely yield the "best" outcomes for patients based upon the available evidence. However, as we have presented earlier, there is often a disconnect between what care providers believe their patients might value most and what truly matters most to patients.

With advancing technology and increases in the number of chronic conditions, it became more common for providers and patients to face treatment decisions where there was no single superior option. Multiple options, each with their own risks and benefits, were possible, which meant a patient's preferences and risk tolerance became important; however, personal preferences and loss aversion were not part of the typical evidence data set. This necessitated the move toward shared decision-making in patient care, in which the former "just the evidence" approach to care is being supplemented by models that favor more interaction with patients and their families. It was therefore inevitable that PROs would need to be incorporated into the decision-making process. However, efforts toward incorporating this data into EHRs, disease registries, and administrative data have only begun in recent years, and mostly in the area of clinical trials.

Patient-centered care, with a focus on evidence-based decision-making, does incorporate some of the broad concepts that have led to the use of PROs, such as providing complete, unbiased, and useful information to patients and their families and encouraging them to participate in the decision-making process and to collaborate with their care providers. However, the earliest patient-centered survey instruments had mostly a customer-service angle. These were primarily satisfaction surveys, focusing on issues such as whether patients were satisfied with the completeness of information they received about their conditions and treatment options, service issues such as wait times, and the level of satisfaction with the quality of care received. This began to change with the advent of medical outcome studies in the 1980s and early 1990s.

3.2 Patient-reported outcome measures

The next step in the evolution of outcomes research was to develop tools that would allow patients to report their perceptions of their health and how they view their outcomes from care and treatment. These surveys began to provide remarkable insight into what patients value most about their health.

The U.S. Food and Drug Administration (2009) defines patient-reported outcome measures (PROMs) as "any report of the status of a patient's (or person's) health condition, health behavior, or experience with healthcare that comes directly from the patient, without interpretation of the patient's response by a clinician or anyone else." Many see the use of PROMs as having advantages beyond traditional provider-centric measures because of their potential to drive behavior change, not only for patients, but for everyone involved in care management, including care providers, healthcare managers, and policymakers. The tools used to collect this information can be paper- or electronic-based and either generic or condition-specific.

3.2.1 Generic PRO tools

One of the earliest generic surveys, and now the most widely used, is the 36-item short form survey known as the SF-36, developed originally by John E. Ware Jr., PhD. Dr. Ware is the founder and chief science officer at the John Ware Research Group and professor and chief of the Division of Outcomes Measurement Science in the Department of Quantitative Health Sciences at the University of Massachusetts Medical School (UMMS).

The medical outcomes studies of the 1990s, in which Ware was deeply involved, asked patients hundreds of questions about their health, their sense of well-being, and their ability to complete their daily activities in the roles they defined for themselves. As these progressed, researchers categorized the questions into eight dimensions that included physical, mental, and social health. Eventually, the list of questions was culled to a few dozen meant to be applicable to all adults, regardless of their medical conditions.

The SF-36 consists of eight scaled scores, which are the weighted sums of the questions in each section, or dimension. The eight sections are

- vitality;
- physical functioning;
- bodily pain;
- general health perceptions;
- physical role functioning;
- emotional role functioning;
- social role functioning; and
- mental health.

Each scale is transformed into a 0–100 scale on the assumption that each question carries equal weight. A lower score indicates a higher level of disability, while a higher score means less disability. The weighted formulas used to calculate the scales are complex, so software is helpful. Age- and gender-adjusted mean values for each scale are available, and norm-based composite scores for physical and mental health can be calculated. Composite scores also range from 0 to 100, with 50 and a standard deviation of ±10 as the normal value.

3.2.2 Condition-specific PRO tools

One example of a condition-specific PRO tool is the Hip Disability and Osteoarthritis Outcome Score (HOOS), which is a questionnaire developed from the Western Ontario and McMaster Universities Osteoarthritis Index (WOMAC). This survey scores the patient's assessment of their hip and associated problems and evaluates symptoms and limitations during therapeutic care. HOOS comprises 40 questions that examine five subscales: pain, symptoms, activity of daily living, sport and recreation function, and hip-related quality of life. The calculation results in a score that ranges from 0 to 100, with higher scores representing better function. The HOOS JR. is a refined six-item survey from the longer version. The complete survey on the refined version is available at multiple locations of the Internet.

The Oswestry Disability Index is one of the earliest PRO Tools, first published by Jeremy Fairbank et al. in *Physiotherapy* in 1980 and then presented with an updated version 20 years later. The index measures the patient's level of disability and estimates the quality of life in a person with low back pain. This PRO questionnaire consists of 10 topics, covering pain intensity, lifting, ability to care for oneself, ability to walk, ability to sit, sexual function, ability to stand, social life, sleep quality, and ability to travel. Each question is scored 0–5, with the first statement being 0 (indicating the least amount of disability) and the last statement scored 5 (indicating most severe). The sum of all of the answers is then multiplied by two to obtain the index. An index score of zero indicates no disability, and 100 is the maximum disability possible.

3.3 Patient-generated outcome measure

A fairly recent development in outcome measurement is patient-generated measures. Here, patients are involved in generating the measurement tool itself and/or participating in creating refinements to an existing tool.

3.3.1 CollaboRATE

The CollaboRATE survey is an example of a patient-generated and PROM. While I was at Dartmouth, several terrific colleagues and I worked to create a practical patient-reported measure of our shared decision-making process by interviewing dozens of patients. We found, to our surprise, that patients were not comfortable with how we were using the words *decision* and *preferences*, because they felt that both decision-making and preferences had different connotations when put into a health care context compared with other aspects of everyday life. Because of this feedback, we began conducting focus groups with patients to help us build items for the questionnaire so they made sense to patients in the healthcare context. After getting consensus on a set of questions, we tested their performance until we were sure that we had solid evidence the questions were measuring shared decision-making, made sense to patients, and performed predictably. This patient-reported survey, which was also patient-generated, is called CollaboRATE.

CollaboRATE is a three-item survey that can be texted to patient's cell phones immediately after their healthcare encounter. These are the three items:

■ How much effort was made to help you understand your health issues?
■ How much effort was made to listen to the things that matter most to you about your health issues?
■ How much effort was made to include what matters most to you in choosing what to do next?

Scoring occurs on a five-point scale, from "no effort was made" up to "every effort was made." The entire process for patients to complete the questionnaire takes less than two minutes.

3.4 Where PROMs are heading

PROMs and their tools have yet to gain widespread clinical use outside of research settings, and many in health care may be unfamiliar with them. Even where PROMs have been implemented, it is still uncommon for a practice or organization to have robust systems and processes in place to disseminate findings, implement tests of change, assess the impact of the change, and share findings across departmentalized service lines. However, steps are being taken to raise awareness of them among healthcare stakeholders.

One example is the effort of the International Consortium for Health Outcomes Measurement (ICHOM), whose mission is to "unlock the potential of value-based health care by defining global Standard Sets of outcome measures that really matter to patients for the most relevant medical conditions and by driving adoption and reporting of these measures worldwide." By the end of 2017, ICHOM met its goals to have published Standard Sets for more than 50% of the global disease burden. ICHOM believes these PROMs will support informed decision-making and improve healthcare quality. They also hope the standards will help reduce healthcare costs by preventing medical errors and unnecessary treatments, and also create a better financial environment for payers so that they spend money on achieving results, not on avoidable costs.

The Hospital Value Purchasing Program, the Merit-Based Incentive Payment System of MACRA, and other payment models encourage care providers to elicit timely feedback on their scores by financially rewarding or punishing them based on aggregated PROMs. The usefulness of this feedback has been disappointing, mostly because of the delay between the time the care is provided and when the provider receives feedback.

3.4.1 Point-of-care PROMs

To help ensure success, some organizations have created methods for accelerating the feedback and learning processes.

These include using app-enabled or web-based surveys for tablets and smart phones. Before their appointments, patients complete the surveys on a device and then the results are fed forward to care providers so they are available during the patient–provider interaction. Using point-of-care PROMs in this way takes some work in building the infrastructure and applications, so this is not yet commonplace. In addition, there are many important nuances in how to deliver and display surveys to patients and how to deliver and display results to the care providers. Then, there is the issue of training care providers to integrate this additional information into their practice.

To summarize, outcome measures have evolved from provider-centric, anatomic, and physiologic measures, to patient-centric measures. Patient-centric measures were first created and used by care providers and became staples of evidence-based medicine and necessary supplements to medical shared decision-making. Patient-reported outcomes grew out of the need to better understand previously unmeasured patient attributes such as preferences, loss aversion, general health perception, and role fulfillment. Patient-reported outcomes can be classified as either generic, which are useful regardless of a patient's diagnosis, or condition-specific, which are specifically built with a single diagnosis in mind. Most recently, patient-centered measures are not only reported by patients, they are being formulated with patients as the guiding participants.

While such systems are not common, some organizations have persisted through the difficulties and have reported substantial improvement to care processes. The improvements stem from using the data to more quickly observe what matters most to the patient and then to orient the patient, provider, and care team around what matters most. In the next chapter, we will examine what the use of PROMs at the point of care looks like.

Bibliography

Barr, P. J., R. Thompson, T. Walsh, S. W. Grande, E. Ozanne, and G. Elwyn. (2014). The psychometric properties of CollaboRATE: A fast and frugal patient-reported measure of shared decision-making process. *Journal of Medical Internet Research* 16, no. 1: e2. doi:10.2196/jmir.3085.

Elwyn, G., P. J. Barr, S. W. Grande, T. Walsh, R. Thompson, and E. Ozanne. (2013). Developing CollaboRATE: A fast and frugal measure of shared decision-making in clinical encounters. *Patient Education and Counseling* 93, no. 1:102–107.

Fairbank, J. C., J. Couper, and J. B. Davies. (1980). The Oswestry low back pain questionnaire. *Physiotherapy* 1980, no. 66:271–273.

Fairbank, J. C. and P. B. Pynsent. (2000). The Oswestry disability index. *Spine 2000* 25, no. 22:2940–2952.

Frampton, S., Guastello, S., Brady, C., Hale, M., Horowitz, S., Bennett Smith, S., Stone, S. (October 2008). *Patient-Centered Care Improvement Guide.* Derby, CT: Planetree.

Kyte, D. G., M. Calvert, P. J. van der Wees, R. Ten Hove, S. Tolan, and J. C. Hill. (2015). An introduction to patient-reported outcome measures (PROMs) in physiotherapy. *Physiotherapy* 101:119–125.

National Quality Forum. (2013, Jan. 10). *Patient-reported outcomes (PROs) in performance measurement.* Washington, DC: National Quality Forum. http://www.qualityforum.org/Publications/2012/12/Patient-Reported_Outcomes_Final_Report.aspx.

U.S. Food and Drug Administration. (2009). Guidance for industry, patient-reported outcome measures: Use in medical product development to support labeling claims. *Federal Registry* 74, no. 35:65132–65133. Available at http://www.fda.gov/downloads/Drugs/GuidanceComplianceRegulatoryInformation/Guidances/UCM193282.pdf.

Chapter 4

Patient-reported measures in action

I have presented the background of patient-reported outcomes, including generic and condition-specific types, as well as the distinctions between patient-centered, patient-reported, and patient-generated. In addition, I have presented the spread of patient-reported outcome measures off the spreadsheets of researchers, out of the data cloud of reimbursement, and into the patient–provider interaction at the point of service.

It is one thing to know the background, types, distinctions, and growth of patient-reported outcomes, but knowing how to use them at the point of service is another thing. A few providers have received training in the use of patient-reported measures at the point of service; however, they have had no training in the interpretation of the patient's scores, let alone any instruction in how to integrate the information into their interactions with a patient.

Even with training on the use of patient-reported outcomes at the point of service, getting started can feel awkward. This is normal, because the process of honing a personalized approach to communicating with a patient feels awkward and slow. It is also common to worry that the therapeutic relationship is diminished in some way as the provider learns to integrate patient-reported outcomes into their practice. However, a provider will not remain awkward or slow forever, and any harm to the therapeutic relationship that may theoretically result from an altered interaction is quickly overcome by the enhanced communication that results from new insights.

The initial awkward feeling is common because the provider is learning a new skill. Although it is common to think of a skill as being something physical, like hitting a baseball or playing the cello, communicating with patients is also a skill. With any skill, developing mastery happens over time and proceeds through several phases (see Table 4.1).

Without prior instruction, the provider did not have an opportunity to develop competency, nor was he/she conscious of his/her incompetence. Upon learning background knowledge regarding a new skill, he/she becomes conscious of his/her incompetence. This is uncomfortable, particularly for a provider who has been in practice for some time. With time, skill level improves toward competence, but only with conscious effort in the practice. If awareness fades, old habits and patterns re-emerge. Over time, the new skill acquires some permanence and no longer requires conscious effort.

In my past role training residents and medical students and my current role as a consultant, many providers have asked to "see and hear" what it is like to use the communication skills outlined in this book. So, here I will provide a fictitious narrative of an initial visit to create a visual

Table 4.1 Phases of learning a new skill

	Awareness Level	Skill Level
Phase 1	Unconscious	Incompetent
Phase 2	Conscious	Incompetent
Phase 3	Conscious	Competent
Phase 4	Unconscious	Competent

and auditory experience as the reader imagines himself/herself in the provider role during the narrative.

4.1 An initial visit

"Thank you for answering those questions on our app. They help us treat you better. Let's take a look at your scores."

"Oh good. I wondered what that was about."

"So, let's start with the big chart here in the middle. Now, the dotted line across the top of the SF-36 box. The dotted line represents a person like you, your age, in good health. I can see that your symptoms have affected you physically as well as emotionally. And glancing over here, under Functional Status, it looks like your function is extremely limited when it comes to sleeping and your social life. Can you tell me more about what's been going on?"

Opening comments like this take less than a minute, but much is accomplished in that time. First, thanking the patient for taking the time to answer the questions is courteous and respectful. Second, reviewing the scores with the patients communicates that the patient's effort to complete the surveys were meaningful. Third, the stage has been set for a nonjudgmental discussion of the total impact—physical, emotional, and social—of the patient's symptoms and their experience in coping with them.

Let's take a look at another data display. In Fig. 4.1, the arrows (not shown on the data display at the clinic but used here to draw your attention) help to highlight what matters most to this particular patient. Looking from bottom arrow to the top, he reports his sleep is extremely limited due to his back pain. His self-reported mental health status is substantially below age—and gender-adjusted norms, indicated by the

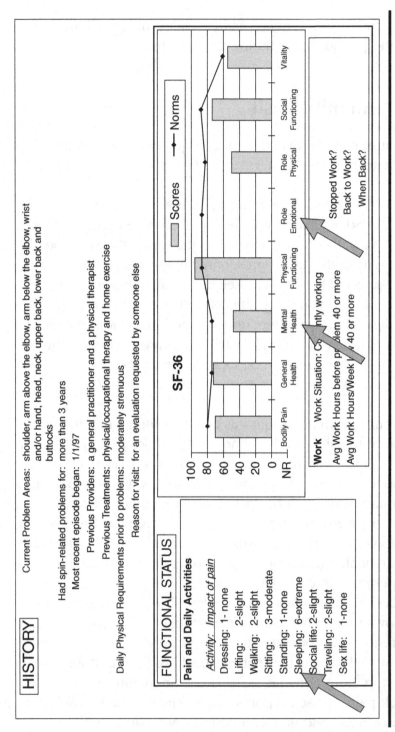

Figure 4.1   Sample Data Display of Patient-Reported Measures

dotted line. And he reports a "Role Emotional" score of zero when the normal value for someone like him is almost 90 out of 100. What do all these data mean?

We each have multiple roles. You might be a son, brother, husband, or a father; a high-school teacher, volunteer firefighter, or marathon runner. For each role, you have personal expectations for what it means to fulfill each one. Each role is important and your quality of life may suffer if you were unable to meet your own expectations.

The role scales, both emotional and physical, are meant to assess your sense of any functional limitations due to your emotional or physical well-being. It is possible to interpret the role emotional score shown in Fig. 4.1 as the patient reporting he is unable to function in his roles due to his emotions.

This is interesting. Recall, the patient is at a spine center for complaints of back pain.

Having a data display like this, where the patient-reported data are immediately available at the point of service, becomes very helpful. At a glance, a provider familiar with the data will identify points of interest or areas of concern within seconds, much like the pattern recognition developed by viewing imaging studies such as a CT scan or MRI.

Much like the CT or MRI image, patient-reported data present a static and incomplete picture. False positives are possible, and more detail is required. Here is what gathering more information sounds like.

> "Thank you for answer those questions on our app. They help us treat you better. Let's take a look at your scores."
> "Oh good. I wondered what that was about."
> "So, let's start with the big chart here in the middle. Now, the dotted line across the top of the SF-36 box. The dotted line represents a person like you, your age, in good health. I can see that your symptoms have affected your sleeping a lot. Is that right?"

"Yes, it sure is."

"OK, that is helpful for me to know. And glancing over here, on the Role Emotional Scale, it looks like it might be difficult to fill your roles, like being a husband, a father, a teacher, etc., because of your emotions. We see this when people have had pain for a long time. Can you tell me more about what's been going on?"

There are many possible replies. Here are a couple possibilities.

■ "Those scores are interesting, but I need to tell you that I've been taking medication for schizophrenia since my early 20s. The medicine is very helpful and while I'm still not functioning as well as I'd like, there have been many times that were much worse."

■ Another patient might reply with escalating agitation: "Well, since this pain began, I haven't been able to work, I can't play with my young son. Hell, I can barely walk the dog. Our money situation is awful and getting worse. My wife seems disappointed with me. Tell you the truth, I don't know if I can take all this for another day!"

The scores on the data dashboard may be the same, but these patients are very different. Their needs are different, and what matters most to a person is as unique as each individual. Their treatments should reflect those unique needs and preferences.

Key phrases incorporating patient-reported measures at the point of service during an initial visit:

■ Thank you for filling this out.
■ It helps us treat you better.
■ Tell me more about this score ...

Chapter 5

Shared decision-making helps find what matters most

Shared decision-making in health care was first mentioned in the literature in 1982, when a presidential commission presented some of the ethical and legal aspects of informed consent in decision-making relationships between providers and patients. However, informed consent is just one of the steps that led to the evolution of shared decision-making as we know it today.

A good, concise definition of shared decision-making in health care can be found in a fact sheet published on the National Learning Consortium's website: "Shared decision making is a key component of patient-centered health care. It is a process in which clinicians and patients work together to make decisions and select tests, treatments and care plans based on clinical evidence that balances risks and expected outcomes with patient preferences and values." This succinct definition belies the complexity of what it can take to get to the point of decision. There are many barriers to successful shared decision-making in health care, including care provider resistance and patient ambivalence.

In 1997, Charles et al. argued that a shared decision-making model should have these four necessary characteristics:

1. At a minimum, both the physician and patient are involved in the treatment decision-making process.
2. Both the physician and patient share information with each other.
3. Both the physician and the patient take steps to participate in the decision-making process by expressing treatment preferences.
4. A treatment decision is made, and both the physician and patient agree on the treatment to implement.

Again, while these are seemingly simple concepts, the process poses challenges for care providers who are new to their implementation. To understand shared decision-making, it is helpful to briefly discuss two other models in healthcare decision-making: paternalistic and informed.

Before the advent of shared decision-making models in the 1980s, the healthcare decision-making relationship among patients and providers was rooted in deference to professional authority, which is the foundation of what is known as the paternalistic model. In this paradigm, care providers generally play the dominant role in treatment and care management decisions. The patient defers to the provider based on several assumptions: (1) that there is usually one best treatment regimen for most conditions, (2) that providers are familiar with the latest and most valid evidence on that preferred regimen, even if it is not their own specialty, (3) that providers will consistently apply that knowledge or refer the patient to another care provider with the appropriate experience, and (4) that their professional concern and code of ethics would guide care providers to put the best interest of their patients before any other concerns.

The first assumption of the paternalistic model, that there is usually one best treatment, has lost relevance as technology has advanced, chronic diseases have become more common, and people are living longer—often with multiple conditions, each with multiple treatment options. Research on variation in health care during the latter part of the previous century began to reveal inexplicably large variations in medical outcomes across relatively small, homogenous regions. These findings cast doubt on the second, third, and fourth assumptions of paternalism, which are that providers are familiar with the latest and most valid evidence on preferred regimens and that they consistently apply that knowledge to the care of patients. Other issues that have contributed to the decline of paternalism in healthcare decision-making include the proliferation of clinical information on the Internet, laws requiring greater provider accountability for informed consent, and the rise of value-based healthcare reimbursement models.

One aspect of the paternalistic and informed models that survives in the shared decision-making models of today is informed consent, which means that a patient provides permission for a course of treatment only after being informed of all of the available treatment/management options. In the paternalistic model, informed consent is more of a legal necessity, with the physician essentially informing the patient of the options and then making the decision on the "best" option for him/her (according to the provider, not the patient) after the patient granted permission to do so.

In both the paternalistic and informed decision models, the exchange of information proceeds in one way, from the provider to the patient. In the paternalistic model, the provider makes the treatment/management decisions, and in the informed model, the patient is left to decide on these. Different from them both, in shared decision-making, information exchange always goes both ways.

Instead of physicians taking a paternalistic approach and making treatment decisions for patients, or an informed model that relegates decisions to patients, a shared decision-making approach involves patients and physicians collaborating, considering options in treatment and management, discussing potential harm and benefit, and then coming to informed personal preferences. It is important to keep in mind when discussing shared decision-making that research has found that some of the terms, such as "options" and "preferences," while common among care providers and researchers, are unfamiliar to many patients in the healthcare setting. It is easy to lapse into the use of these clinical terms when talking with patients, but the terms may not be interpreted in the intended manner. This is why it is helpful to have a simple model to guide the collaborative deliberation.

While providing the patient with information on all available courses of treatment is a vital component of today's shared decision-making models, there is much more to the process. Studies consistently show that patients make different choices when they are well informed. Research also shows that there is often a large difference between what patients want and what healthcare providers believe their patients want. For these reasons, it is not enough to simply inform the patient—the care provider must add collaboration and deliberation to the process in order to come to the best shared decisions.

5.1 The 3-Talk Model of shared decision-making

The 3-Talk Model of engaging patients in discussions about their health care is centered on choices, options, and decisions. It proceeds through three steps, from Team Talk to Option Talk to Decision Talk.

In Team Talk, the care provider assures the patient that they are part of a team and will not be left alone to make decisions. Option Talk is the point at which options, and the pros and cons of each, are discussed. In Decision Talk, preferences, or "what matters most" to the patient, are determined and explored. Because there are many facets to the 3-Talk Model, let's examine each of these steps more closely.

5.1.1 Team Talk

Team Talk is an invitation from the healthcare provider to the patient to become part of the patient's healthcare team. The goal of this talk is to relieve some of the intimidation and trepidation that people of all backgrounds can feel in a doctor's office or in the hospital. Real teamwork can happen only when patients feel their involvement and feedback in the decision-making process is just as important as the provider's.

5.1.2 Option Talk

In Option Talk, the care provider describes care management and treatment options, pointing out the potential risks and benefits of each. If the state of the science is incomplete in a certain area, the provider informs the patient that the issue is being studied but that more information is needed to assess what is best for each person. In this phase, in which the patient can become uneasy, it is important to pause between options as they are presented to note the patient's reactions. If you notice the patient is uncomfortable or puzzled, tell them you are aware of this and then prompt them for concerns or questions.

During the discussion, write the options down and ensure you adequately explain all of the pros and cons of each, while avoiding the natural inclination to emphasize pros over cons or vice versa. Patient decision-support tools can be helpful here. Decision boards, option grids, issue cards, and other decision-support aids can be incorporated as appropriate during the encounter. Beyond the office visit, videos and links to helpful websites can provide information and support that can help patients collaborate with other people in their lives.

At the end of the Team Talk, ensure that you summarize the options and your understanding of the patient's informed preferences to confirm that both of you have arrived at the same place. This sets the stage for Decision Talk.

5.1.3 Decision Talk

Before you decide to proceed with the Decision Talk step, ensure the patient is ready to decide. They may need time to talk with friends or family, or they may want a second opinion. If they ask for your opinion as to the course of action, share your thoughts with them, but continue to guide them back to what is most important to them. They will often ask for your opinion because they are overwhelmed or ambivalent about their options. Ask them what is troubling them about making the decision, which can help elicit statements about what matters most to them.

Keep in mind that Team Talk, Option Talk, and Decision Talk frequently can all occur during a single session, but that they do not always come together during one visit. Getting through all three steps may require multiple sessions, and sometimes you may have to start back at square one.

Beyond providing information, patient collaboration is critical in eliciting informed preferences going forward and integrating them into the chosen treatment. In the next chapter, we will present more detail and scenarios that highlight how the 3-Talk Model can be successfully implemented in shared decision-making.

Bibliography

Charles, C., A. Gafni, and T. Whelan. (1997). Shared decision-making in the medical encounter: What does it mean? (Or it takes at least two to tango). *Social Science & Medicine* 44, no. 5:681–692. doi:10.1016/S0277-9536(96)00221-3.

Charles, C., A. Gafni, and T. Whelan. (1999). Decision-making in the physician-patient encounter: Revisiting the shared treatment decision-making model. *Social Science & Medicine* 49:651–661. doi:10.1016/S0277-9536(99)00145-8.

Elwyn G., D. Frosch, R. Thomson, et al. (2012). Shared decision making: A model for clinical practice. *Journal of General Medicine* 27, no. 10:1361–1367. Published online May 23, 2012. doi: 10.1007/s11606-012-2077-6.

National Learning Consortium. (2013). Fact sheet: Shared decision making. https://www.healthit.gov/sites/default/files/nlc_shared_decision_making_fact_sheet.pdf.

President's Commission for the Study of Ethical Problems in Medicine and Biomedical and Behavioral Research. (1982). *Making health care decisions: The ethical and legal implications of informed consent in the patient–practitioner relationship.* Washington, DC. http://hdl.handle.net/10822/811956.

Wennberg, J. E. (2010). *Tracking medicine: A researcher's quest to understand healthcare.* Oxford, UK: Oxford University Press.

Chapter 6

Shared decision-making in action

Discussing patient preferences and treatment options does not come naturally for most of us. We are experts in our own treatments, have years of experience with hundreds of patients, and know the relevant scientific literature. We may even have contributed to it. Even so, it is becoming harder and harder to keep up with advances in treatments. Many conditions have multiple treatments within a single specialty. While the treatments all aim to improve the patient's condition or quality of life, their risk profiles can vary dramatically. And while humans share an aversion to risk, there is a wide range of individual tolerances. Risk tolerance, lifestyle, and available support systems are a few of the items that may influence a patient's preference for one treatment option over another. Providers need a way to communicate with patients in order to decipher a patient's preferences and what matters most to them.

Using patient-reported outcomes at the point of service helps providers identify what matters most to the patient in front of him/her now. Describing treatment options and deciphering a patient's preferences effectively is a process.

Mulley and colleagues have likened the process to arriving at a diagnosis.

Providers make a medical diagnosis by evaluating a patient's primary complaints, past history, exam findings, and test results. A preference diagnosis can be thought of similarly. Providers work with their patients to identify what matters most to them, discuss the risks and benefits of the available treatment options, and support the patient as needed through the decision-making process.

Elwyn described this as a collaborative deliberation process. The process consists of three parts. Conceptually, the 3-Talk Model is linear, with distinct boundaries consisting of a talk to create a team between the provider and patient, a talk to discuss options, and a talk to discuss and review the jointly made decision. In the space between the Option Talk and the Decision Talk, the patient preferences may change.

When learning of options, patients will frequently have an initial preference for one or another. If asked why they have that preference, they commonly say things such as "I heard about that on the TV," or "my neighbor had something similar and that worked for him." It is also common for preferences to change as patients learn more about the risks and benefits of each option and compare those with their own risk

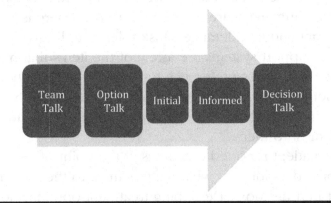

Figure 6.1   The 3-Talk Model

tolerance, lifestyle, and support network. In this way, a patient's preferences change from initial to informed. A preference diagnosis is not correct until the patient is informed. Arriving at a preference diagnosis before this point is akin to arriving at a medical diagnosis without a clinical exam or test results. You might be right occasionally, but a misdiagnosis is likely most of the time.

How often does a preference misdiagnosis occur? It is difficult to measure, in part because the term is not widely used. Still, based on what we can infer, preference misdiagnoses are common. We deduce this by observing the frequency with which patients change their treatment preferences after learning more about their treatment options. Researchers have consistently found that 20% to 40% of patients presenting with an initial treatment preference choose another treatment after becoming more informed. After being informed of the risks and benefits associated with their options, men with prostate diseases choose surgery 40% less often; patients with a disc herniation in their lower spine choose surgery 30% less often; and patients with lumbar spinal stenosis choose surgery 30% more often when compared with patients who did not receive complete information about treatment options.

Other findings demonstrate how poorly care providers do when asked to estimate which patients will want one treatment or another. For example, Lee et al. (2010) asked surgical oncologists to estimate what percentage of their patients would rate "saving my breast" as a high priority. Overall, the surgeons estimated 71% of their patients would give that outcome a high priority, but only 17% of patients rated it as one of their priorities.

In another example, Canadian researchers interviewed orthopedic surgeons after asking them to review the overall health, physical exam findings, imaging results, and treatment outcomes for a cohort of patients with osteoarthritis of the knee. The researchers asked the surgeons to identify the patient records with findings consistent with the type of patient who would be likely to prefer knee replacement surgery. The researchers then assessed those particular patients' treatment preference. Of all the patients deemed eligible for and likely to prefer surgery, only 15% chose to proceed with the procedure.

Should we take these results to mean care providers are completely inept in their communications with patients? I do not think so. Rather, these results speak to the fact that care providers are rushed and have not been trained in the communication skills needed to make a preference diagnosis both effectively and efficiently.

Most care providers, on their best days, are able to communicate well and deliberate collaboratively with patients. In my experience, they even enjoy it. However, "best days" are rare. More often, they are feeling ever-growing pressures to do more and to assume responsibility for outcomes they feel are beyond their control. They are late to where they need to be now, and behind on what needs to be done overall. All these factors makes it easier for us as providers to kindly tell a patient what we can do for them or what he/she needs to do for himself/herself and then leave it up to him/her to decide which path to take.

Meanwhile, shared decision-making academics outline a cumbersome process of communication that is disseminated through peer-reviewed publications, which are read primarily by academics. This helps those of us in academia feel as though we have specialized knowledge but does little to train the care providers who interact with patients.

A "good enough" process is needed, one that is also more easily learned and adaptable to each unique patient, regardless of the setting. The process should not take too long or require too many additional resources—something fast and frugal. The 3-Talk Model was designed for such a purpose. Below is an example of a patient and a care provider collaborating over treatment options. I have organized the text into the Team Talk, Option Talk, and Decision Talk components that make up the 3-Talk Model. In reality, the talks are seldom this linear and are often iterative, but a good understanding of the basic model makes it easier to customize as needed.

6.1 Team Talk

"Thank you, doctor, for explaining my diagnosis.

You're welcome, Mr. Jones. Now, with this condition, we are fortunate to have several treatments to choose from. Each one has its own set of risks and benefits. I know the science about them, and I have seen hundreds of patients like you, but I have only just met you. I will need your help to understand what matters most to you so we can figure out the best treatment given your specific preferences. We'll need to be a team."

In those five sentences, the care provider has set the stage for a collaborative deliberation of the available options.

This is important because we know that even highly educated, wealthy, professionals can be intimidated in healthcare settings. Patients can be reluctant to ask questions or give their opinion out of the worry it might upset their care provider and ultimately affect their care or their interactions with other staff members. For these reasons, we need to let patients know their participation in the team is welcomed and helpful.

6.2 Option Talk

"OK, doctor, I understand there are options and you want to know how I feel about them.

Right. So don't hesitate to ask questions or for
more information. I'm going to use this piece of
paper to make a little grid so we can compare
treatments A, B, and C side by side. Over here, on
the left, I'm going to write down a couple topics
that many patients like you have asked in the past.
I'll leave room for your specific questions too.
One of the first questions most people ask is,
"How long until I feel better?" Well, with
treatment A ..."

While discussing the options, the care provider assesses the
patient's body language while listening to questions and
comments. Body language is usually the first sign to appear
if the patient starts to feel overwhelmed or confused. If body
language clues are missed, an overwhelmed patient will often
ask, "What would you do?"

When a patient asks, "What would you do?" it is usually a
signal of uncertainty. It is seldom a capitulation of his/her
autonomy. The patient usually needs more information or
more time, or both. So, ask if there is anything that is unclear.
Ask if it would help to take more time or to talk things over
with a family member.

Researchers do not usually encourage care providers to
answer the "What would you do" question for fear that an
answer will bias the patient's decision. But most of us are not
participating in research or following a specific protocol. It is
OK to use professional judgment. You might say something
like this:

"It's interesting you ask what I would do. I'm still
trying to learn more about what matters most to you,
so I'm not sure how alike or different we might be.
Having said that, if I were faced with these choices, I
would choose this option, here. I would choose it
because there are certain things that matter most to

me, like … How does that match up to what matters
for you?"

Decision aids are pre-made grids, pamphlets, and even videos
that work through the common questions patients have as
well as the risks and benefits of the relevant treatment options.
These can be helpful when more time is required or when the
patient wants to discuss material with their family or friends.
Shared decision-making experts have made decision aids for
many common conditions with multiple treatment options.
The aids can be found on the Internet by searching for
shared decision-making decision aids for the condition that
interests you.

However, overreliance on decision aids can be a problem.
When used properly, they can augment the Option Talk very
nicely, but it is not sufficient to hand them out as if they were
parting gifts. The Team Talk is still needed, and assessing
body language during even abbreviated Option Talk can
provide a lot of insight into what is worrying or calming a
particular patient.

Numeracy is another topic to consider when comparing
options. Confusion is common when talking about risk and
the ratios we use to describe it and when we confront patients
with probabilities, percentages, odds, and other ratios as they
move from initial to informed preferences.

I will share an example to show how easy it is for even
highly educated care providers to be confused with ratios.
In one study, researchers asked practicing care providers to
predict the likelihood that a patient who tested positive for
a disease really did have the disease. Now, they did not
have to be precise. They were simply asked whether the
likelihood was closer to 30% or 70%. They were given all
the information needed to figure out a precise answer—the
disease had a 10% base rate, 80% sensitivity, and 80%
specificity, but they only had to determine whether the true
positive would be closer to 30% or 70%. Among this highly

educated sample, less than one-third chose the correct response.

You would think that with only two responses, if they had simply guessed, 50% would have been correct. The participants obviously tried to calculate "something," but it did not work.

Here is another famous example. A ball and a bat, together, cost $1.10. The bat costs $1 more than the ball. How much does the ball cost?

Now, most people—even healthy, caffeinated economists—say the ball costs $0.10, but that is wrong. If the ball costs $0.10, then the bat, which costs $1 more than the ball, would cost $1.10, and together they would be $1.20. Human brains like to think fast and default toward the easy answer that makes immediate sense. But think slowly and clearly, and you will see the ball must cost $0.05. Then, the bat would be $1.05, and the total would be $1.10.

The point I want to make is that our brains are prone to these types of errors. All human brains—even highly trained, healthy, and caffeinated brains—make these mistakes. When we understand that these biases and misjudgements are ingrained, we can take steps to overcome them by using additional visual clues such as tables and charts.

Another potential point of confusion comes from the two ways we compare two ratios: the absolute difference between them or the relative difference.

In Table 6.1, we see that among the patients receiving the new treatment, roughly seven in 1,000 suffer adverse events,

Table 6.1   Risk of adverse event

	New Treatment	Old Treatment
Adverse events	7	15
Total treated	983	1028
	0.007	0.015

while among patients receiving the old treatment, the number is 15 in 1,000. To calculate the absolute difference, subtract the low from the high; we find that the absolute risk reduction is 0.008.

The relative difference will look more impressive. The relative difference is found by dividing new (0.007) by the old (0.015), which yields a relative risk reduction of 0.0467, or nearly 50%.

A salesman would likely use the relative reduction because it feels more impressive. As care providers, it is wise to emphasize the absolute rates. Still, even when we use absolute rates, it can be hard to get your head around numbers like eight in 1,000.

Our goal is to help our patients weigh both the benefits and risks of all their options. To do this, we want to make sure we provide balanced information. One way to do this is to make sure we frame risks in terms of both benefits and harms; however, we can easily overwhelm patients with multiple comparisons. Displaying the information in a table can help.

Table 6.2, for instance, is easily drawn if you can recall the appropriate numbers for the test or treatment being discussed. We want to provide a balanced view of risks and benefits. The decision to have or forgo a screening exam can be one of the hardest to discuss with a patient. It can be challenging

Table 6.2 Results of screening for prostate cancer

	100 Without Screening	100 With Screening
Benefits		
How many die from prostate cancer?	1	1
How many die from any cause?	21	21
Harms		
How many false alarms?	0	16
How many diagnosed and treated unnecessarily?	0	2

because the risks associated with a screening exam and early disease detection may not be obvious. Care providers need to explain that some individuals will have a false alarm. The initial test will be positive, but the follow-up, definitive test will be negative. In addition, a number of patients will suffer side effects from treatments after a positive screening exam. The side effects can sometimes be significant, and some patients may choose to forgo the treatment because of them.

Icon arrays such as Fig. 6.2 can be helpful in this scenario, where we are dealing with multiple ratios for multiple outcomes. The arrays are easy to draw, but some care providers find it easier to have handouts pre made for common screening exams.

Visual aids are a powerful way to help patients quickly grasp important content. This is especially true as the tradeoffs to consider become more numerous. You can use pre-made decision cards, options grids, or a similar tool within the treatment encounter. The Harding Center and the Mayo Clinic both have online tools to help convey this information outside of the clinical encounter. Either constructed as needed or pre-made, the icon array can help you demonstrate that, in this instance, the benefit from this screening exam is small for the patient.

Communicating risks is a part of Option Talk. It is important to remember that human brains are prone to making biases and misjudgments when we talk about probabilities, so it is a good idea to check how well you have communicated. Ask your patient, "When you go home, how are you going to explain your options to your family and friends?"

6.3 Decision Talk

After the Team Talk, the Option Talk, an assessment of body language, and checking comprehension of the risks and

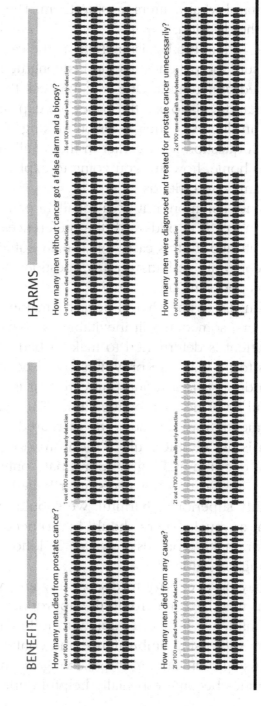

Prostate Cancer Early Detection

BENEFITS

How many men died from prostate cancer?

1 out of 100 men died without early detection

1 out of 100 men died with early detection

How many men died from any cause?

21 out of 100 men died without early detection

21 out of 100 men died with early detection

HARMS

How many men without cancer got a false alarm and a biopsy?

0 out of 100 men died without early detection

16 of 100 men died with early detection

How many men were diagnosed and treated for prostate cancer unnecessarily?

0 of 100 men died without early detection

2 of 100 men died with early detection

Figure 6.2   Benefits and Harms of Prostate Cancer Screening

benefits for the available options, most patients will understand what matters most to them. They are ready to make the decision.

Your role in the Decision Talk, as the care provider, is to make sure the patient's decision is congruent with his/her informed preferences. One way to check the patient's understanding is to ask the patient to explain back to you the main drivers of their decision-making. To do so, you can tweak a question used earlier in the 3-Talk model: "When you go home, how are you going to explain your decision to your family and friends?"

It is not common, but occasionally a patient will make a decision that is at odds with the preferences identified just moments ago. In this case, it is usually sufficient to point out the incongruity and answer any questions or concerns if there is persisting uncertainty.

When discussing shared decision-making with care providers, someone will inevitably ask what should be done if a patient is determined to make a bad choice. The fear seems to be that care providers could be at the mercy of a demanding patient requesting care that is known to be harmful or of no therapeutic value. This question belies a fundamental misunderstanding of shared decision-making, which is usually the fault of the instructor! The process of shared decision-making is appropriate only when there are two or more options of similar benefit. If one treatment is clearly superior or harmful, we should inform the patient as much. There should be no need for a shared decision-making process for, say, childhood vaccinations or smoking cessation!

It may be necessary to discuss any ambivalence the patient may have regarding the appropriate action and his/her confidence in his/her ability to follow through with the action. Addressing ambivalence and confidence is best done using motivational interviewing techniques. These techniques become especially helpful during follow-up visits because it is during that time when patients tell us if they were able to complete the treatment plan agreed upon at the prior visit and what effect their efforts had in addressing what matters most to them. Addressing ambivalence and confidence during follow-up visits is the topic of the next chapter.

Key Phrases in the 3-Talk Model of Shared Decision-Making

■ Team Talk

- "You're welcome, Mr. Jones. Now, with this condition, we are fortunate to have several treatments to choose from. Each one has its own set of risks and benefits. I know the science about them, and I've seen hundreds of patients like you, but I've only just met you. I'll need your help to understand what matters most to you so we can figure the best treatment given your specific preferences. We'll need to be a team."

■ Option Talk

- "Don't hesitate to ask questions or for more information. I'm going to use this piece of paper to make a little grid so we can compare treatments A, B, and C side by side. Over here, on the left, I'm going to write down a couple topics that many patients like you have asked in the past. I'll leave room for your specific questions too. One of the first questions most people ask is 'How long until I feel better.' Well, with treatment A ..."
- "It's interesting you ask what I would do. I'm still trying to learn more about what matters most to you, so I'm not sure how alike or different we might be. Having said that, if I were faced with these choices, I

would choose this option, here. I would choose it because there are certain things that matter most to me, like ... How does that match up to what matters for you?"

- "When you go home, how are you going to explain your options to your family and friends?"

◾ Decision Talk

- "When you go home, how are you going to describe your decision to your family and friends?"

Bibliography

Elwyn, G., P. J. Barr, S. W. Grande, et al. (2013). Developing Collabo-RATE: A fast and frugal measure of shared decision-making in clinical encounters. *Patient Education & Counseling* 93, no. 1:102–107.

Elwyn, G., A. Lloyd, C. May, et al.(2014). Collaborative deliberation: A model for patient care. *Patient Education and Counseling* 97, no. 2:158–164.

Frosch, D. L., S. G. May, K. S. Rendle, et al.(2012). Authoritarian physicians and patients' fear of being labeled "difficult" among key obstacles to shared decision-making. *Health Affairs* 31, no. 5:1030–1038.

Kahnamen, D. (2011). *Thinking, fast and slow.* New York: Farrar, Straus and Giroux.

Lee, M. K., D. Y. Noh, S. J. Nam, et al. (2010). Association of shared decision-making with type of breast cancer surgery: A cross-sectional study. *BMC Health Services Research* 10:48.

Mulley, A., C. Trimble, and G. Elwyn. (2012). *Patient preferences matter: Stop the silent misdiagnosis.* London: The King's Fund.

Reyna, V. F. (2008). Theories of medical decision making and health: An evidence-based approach. *Medical Decision Making* 28, no. 6:829–833.

Chapter 7

Motivational interviewing helps find what matters most

Working with patients to achieve medically indicated behavior change is one of the greatest challenges in care management for chronic conditions. A major barrier to overcome is ambivalence—the patient's mixed feelings or hesitation about adhering to a course of treatment and lifestyle changes. A major source of hesitation is the patient's self-efficacy and confidence in their own ability to successfully implement a change. Motivational interviewing is a communication technique care providers can employ to break through ambivalence and increase confidence to help patients make needed change.

Motivational interviewing is a toolkit of patient-centered counseling techniques that got its start more than 30 years ago in the substance abuse and addiction fields, where changing long-term client behavior is critical to success. As chronic conditions have become more prevalent in our population, motivational interviewing has been increasingly engaged to improve patient involvement in care processes. Drs. William

R. Miller and Stephen Rollnick are considered the pioneers of this method of eliciting positive behavioral changes, which they say works by "activating a patient's own motivation for change and adherence to treatment."

Over the past three decades, motivational interviewing has been the subject of clinical trials covering a wide range of behavioral change challenges. Though not all trials have been positive, many have documented successes, including reducing unprotected sex and needle sharing, increasing exercise and healthy eating, improving adherence to treatment and medication regimens, improving glycemic control, and decreasing drug and alcohol use. Several best-practice care models for chronic conditions, including the Chronic Care Model (CCM) from the MacColl Center (with support from the Robert Wood Johnson Foundation), and the Guided Care Model, which originated with Dr. Chad Boult of Johns Hopkins University, now incorporate motivational interviewing.

7.1 Overcoming ambivalence and increasing confidence

People know that smoking causes lung cancer, heart disease, and other life-threatening medical conditions. They know that overeating, in combination with a sedentary lifestyle, can cause obesity and a host of comorbidities. Care providers might think it would be enough to remind patients of these health risks and say, "Stop doing this to yourself," and then patients would change their behavior. But this approach is often unsuccessful, because ambivalence gets in the way. Patients can feel overwhelmed about the life changes that would be required to control their disease. They can also feel insecure about their ability to succeed at the effort. The challenge for the clinician is to avoid trying to aggressively direct the patient toward certain behaviors and then blaming the patient if the behavior change is not immediate or perfect.

Researchers have found that for most people, it is not that they are unmotivated to change their behavior or to live a healthier life, but they simply need to discover what their primary motivations are and they need to feel confident that their efforts will succeed. Clinicians need to help their patients realize and unlock the motivation inside of them and to build confidence. This is where motivational interviewing can help.

The goals of motivational interviewing are to instill hope, confidence, and action, and to empower patients to change their health choices and behaviors. Miller, Rollnick, and Butler explain it this way:

> Motivational interviewing is not a technique for tricking people into doing what they do not want to do. Rather, it is a skillful clinical style for eliciting from patients their own good motivations for making behavior changes in the interest of their health. It involves guiding more than directing, dancing rather than wrestling, listening at least as much as telling. The overall "spirit" has been described as collaborative, evocative, and honoring of patient autonomy.

7.2 Processes of motivational interviewing

The four processes of motivational interviewing are Engaging, Focusing, Evoking, and Planning. Although these processes are not linear, engagement is generally considered a necessary first step before the processes leading to behavior change can begin. The following describes each of the concepts.

7.2.1 Engaging

The concept of reflective listening helps in this important step, where the clinician is developing rapport, reducing defensiveness, and helping to relieve any ambivalence the patient may have about the clinician's role in the process. Those who practice reflective listening are demonstrating that they are interested in what a person has said about their motivations for behavior change and are inviting the person to elaborate on them. Showing empathy in this way develops a helpful relationship and encourages the person to explore and expand on their motivations for change.

7.2.2 Focusing

In this process, the clinician and the patient are working together to target the behaviors that need to change and concentrating on finding clear direction and goals for that change. The Focusing process is also meant to determine the goals of the patient and how far they are along the road toward attaining them. This is also where the clinician determines whether the patient's and clinician's goals are aligned so they are not starting off working at cross purposes.

7.2.3 Evoking

The Evoking process elicits the patient's internal motivations for change using "Change Talk." In Evoking, the clinician needs to be mindful of avoiding the "righting reflex," which is the impulse to correct or direct someone with unsolicited advice. In Evoking, the clinician must assume that somewhere inside the patient are personal solutions for overcoming ambivalence that can be drawn out in a nonconfrontational way, preventing the door of resistance from being slammed shut.

7.2.4 Planning

The Planning process involves committing to change and creating a specific plan to accomplish it. Planning only occurs after the clinician and patient establish a meaningful engagement with shared goals for change and the patient is appropriately motivated to make the change.

7.3 Techniques to facilitate the processes

Five nonconfrontational counseling techniques are often employed in motivational interviewing:

- Expressing empathy
- Developing discrepancy
- Avoiding argumentation
- Rolling with resistance
- Supporting self-efficacy

Let's break these down in the context of how motivational interviewing works.

7.3.1 Expressing empathy

Patients are more open to suggestions for change when they feel their fears, challenges, and needs related to necessary lifestyle and health changes are understood and accepted. Reflective listening and a non-judgmental mindset are essential tools for expressing empathy.

7.3.2 Developing discrepancy

The clinician should develop discrepancy between the patient's goals and their current behavior. This discrepancy is not presented in a confrontational or judgmental way. Rather, the clinician should subtly make the patient aware of how their current behavior differs from the ideal path they need to be on, and what the consequences may be if necessary changes are not made.

7.3.3 Avoiding argumentation

Motivational interviewing requires collaboration with the patient, so conflict and disagreement are avoided. Clinicians should move with patients toward the need for positive change rather than trying to convince them that a problem exists and telling them what they need to do about it.

7.3.4 Rolling with resistance

In order to avoid a confrontational or combative tone, the clinician needs to "roll" with the patient's resistance rather than challenging it. Reflective listening continues to be vital in this area, as the clinician seeks to bring the patient's perspective into greater focus and offer alternatives to overcoming the obstacle.

7.3.5 Supporting self-efficacy

If patients feel they are successfully self-managing their health, they will be more likely to continue positive behaviors. Clinicians can support a patient's positive view of their self-management through affirming their progress toward healthy behavior change with positive feedback and celebrating accomplishments.

Bibliography

Miller, W. R. and S. Rollnick. (1991). *Motivational interviewing: Preparing people to change addictive behavior.* New York: Guilford Press.

Chapter 8

Motivational interview in action

As I have mentioned, reflective listening plays a prominent role in motivational interviewing. This technique seeks to understand the patient's motivations and confidence level to determine where his/her ambivalence lies and what might be needed to improve his/her confidence level, and it then reflects these ideas back to the patient to confirm that the clinician correctly understands his/her perspectives about the issues. This prompts the patient to struggle with their ambivalence and identify perceived barriers that are decreasing their confidence.

Examples of open-ended questions that can start Change Talk and help the client overcome their ambivalence include:

- "Why is it important for you to stop smoking?"
- "What do you like and not like about smoking?"
- "How would you go about stopping smoking?"

8.1 An example of motivational interviewing during a follow-up visit

An initial visit with a patient typically ends with a treatment plan, and we use the follow-up visit to assess the effects of that treatment approach. This is especially true in the case of chronic conditions. The patient may be better, worse, unchanged, or any of those with a new complaint. The patient's status at the follow-up visit may be the patient's response to the treatment, experience of negative effects or a paradoxical response from the treatment, or the result of the patient not carrying out the treatment.

I recommend using a semi-structured approach to the follow-up visit in order to sort through the possible relation-ships between the treatment plan and the patient's current status. The first step is to compare current patient-reported outcomes with those reported at the initial visit, so it helps to start with "Thank you for filling this out. It helps us treat you better. Let's look at how your scores today compared to your originals." The key to this step is to confirm that the scores displayed generally match the patient's experience.

Suppose that the patient reports a higher pain score. The provider can respond with this:

> "It looks like your pain score has gone up a bit, your mental health score has gone down, and your ability to complete all your roles is a bit more limited due to your emotions. Does that seem right?"

It is important to assess the situation more fully before jumping to conclusions or changing the treatment approach. Is the apparent worsening due to the treatment? Are new factors coming into play?

The second step, then, is to review the treatment plan. "The last time you were here, we decided on treatment ABC." The patient should be nodding in agreement as they recall the initial visit. A simple question follows: "Have you had a chance to try it?" This is an important question because it determines which of two paths the remainder of the visit will follow.

In the first possible path, the follow-up visit becomes a problem-solving session if the patient replies, "No, I haven't been able to complete the treatment." This happens because there are barriers for the patient. What are the barriers? What is needed to overcome them? It is important to remember the relationship between the treatment and the patient's worsening complaints remains unclear at this point. The treatment may still be effective if the barriers can be overcome. When this question is overlooked, which happens frequently, the default decision is to change course because the patient is worse. The new treatment is often more intensive, extensive, and costly than the original. The added costs may not be needed if the barriers can be removed and the true benefits of the treatment are realized.

The second path unfolds if the patient replies, "Yes, I've been able to complete the treatment," the immediate follow-up is neither positive nor negative, but simply "What have you found?" This open-ended question allows the patient to describe the effects of the treatment. Possible responses include "I've found treatment ABC works great and am much better"; "I've found it works a bit, but not enough"; "I don't think it has made any difference"; and "I think it is making me worse."

Treatment choices emerge by asking open-ended questions and listening to the patient's response. Is it appropriate to continue on the same plan, try something new, or problem-solve to help the patient overcome any ambivalence, lack of confidence, lack of resources, or lack of ability to complete the care plan?

A collaborative approach to decision-making is best when the patient and care provider are faced with multiple compelling treatment options. The 3-Talk Model, described earlier, helps to make certain the patient understands the risks and benefits of the choices and makes an informed decision.

After making the decision to either continue treatment ABC with some modifications or to try treatment XYZ, it is helpful to gauge the patient's confidence level regarding the new plan.

"Now that we've decided on this course of treatment, how confident are you regarding your ability to do it? Zero means completely lacking confidence and 10 means completely confident." It is important to check the patient's body language as well as to listen. Confident looks different from unconfident. A score of eight or higher, along with a confident demeanor, is the goal. Here, you are engaging with the patient and letting him know you want to build on the working relationship you have previously established.

Any patient response to the confidence question with a score less than eight or an appearance lacking in confidence calls for a follow-up question. "What is needed to get your score to eight or higher and for you to feel confident enough that someone else could see your belief in your ability just by looking at you?" Here, you are helping him/her to focus on what he/she needs to succeed.

At this point, depending on the patient's response, you may need to help the patient focus on what is most important for success at this particular point.

Imagine the fourth appointment, when the patient shows up and reports, "Yes, I've tried the treatment. No, it is not working. Here's what I think I need." With motivational interviewing, the sessions become action-oriented, and a collaborative, problem-solving focus develops that improves self-efficacy and subtly trains the patient to understand that you are expecting their participation.

After an initial learning curve, visits become shorter, and there are fewer wasted sessions. Motivational interviewing is not confined to follow-up visits, and shared decision-making not to the initial session. Most shared decision-making research has focused on a single decision and one point in time, such as surgery or not for lumbar disc herniation.

The key statements, actions, and questions for results-focused meetings are:

1. "Thank you for filling this out. It helps us treat you better. Let's look at how your scores today compare to your originals."
2. "The last time we were here, we discussed ..."
   a. Assess body language
3. "Have you had a chance to try it?"
   a. Listen
4. "What have you found?"
   a. Listen more
5. Collaboratively create a plan going forward
   a. Try using the 3-Talk Model
6. Ask, "How confident are you about this plan?"
   a. Listen and assess body language
7. If needed, ask, "What needs to happen for you to be very confident?"
   a. Listen and assess body language

Bibliography

Miller, W. R. and S. Rollnick. (1991). *Motivational interviewing: Preparing people to change addictive behavior.* New York: Guilford Press.

Rollnick, S., W. R. Miller, and C. C. Butler. (2008). *Motivational interviewing in health care: Helping patients change behavior.* New York: The Guilford Press.

Chapter 9

Putting the elements together in practice

Patient-reported outcome measures have come a long way in their level of acceptance during the past 150 years, and great strides have been made in their development over the past three decades. In this first section of the book, I have examined the evolution of PROMs and proceeded through implementation, employing various proven methods to collect the necessary data and optimize our use of them.

9.1 Applying the care team model

In *Navigating to Value in Healthcare*, I described a cost-allocation method commonly associated with value-based care: time-driven, activity-based costing. It involves mapping the process of care from a patient's perspective. For example, a patient first enters a clinic and checks in with a receptionist, and then spends some time in the waiting room. Eventually, the patient is escorted back through the clinic to an exam room and is visited by one or more care providers. After the clinical encounter, the patient exits the clinic and visits the same, or another, receptionist to schedule necessary tests, treatments, and follow-up visits. Using the time-driven, activity-based costing method, each stop along the patient's path creates a node. The string of nodes represents a care process. The process map includes the location of each node, personnel involved, time spent waiting between actions, and time spent with each member of the care team, along with any supplies needed by the patient. Each node can further be classified as value-added or non-value-added. The process map representing the current state is then optimized to create an ideal future state.

Value is increased by seeking ways to improve the patient's outcome and experience. This is accomplished by looking for ways to remove non-value-added steps and redesigning any steps that unnecessarily add costs or do not improve outcomes. A note of caution is needed here because it is possible to dive so deeply into each step and time estimate that the overall plot is lost. The result can be a room of administrators, care providers, and consultants meeting weekly over several months and incurring great costs, in an attempt to shave seconds off of a process in one facility.

Three questions will typically lead to the most significant improvements in the care process. First, where should the work be done? Operating and emergency rooms are more expensive than clinical rooms, which are more expensive than waiting areas, administrative offices, or sites off the hospital or clinical campus. Second, who should be doing the work at each node? Is a surgeon needed for the task or a social worker who has been trained to meet the needs at hand? This is another way of asking if we are using each member of the care team to the height of his/her training and skills. Third, how should the work be done? Does each task have to be done in person? Can it be done via phone or videoconference? Can the process be made more efficient?

Of the three questions, the largest cost reductions hide in the examination of personnel and location.

This brief diversion into cost allocation is important because it raises questions such as "Is a clinical exam room the best location, and are physicians the optimal personnel for shared decision-making and motivational interviewing processes?" For most, the reflexive response is "No, physicians are not the optimal personnel for these tasks. Other team members, including social workers, behavioral therapists, and chaplains, may have greater aptitude for, and more training in, interpersonal communication."

While it is true that physicians are not the only team members who review patient-reported outcomes and participate in shared decision-making and motivational interviewing processes with patients, there are several considerations to examine before launching a new workflow designed to harness the interpersonal skills of other care providers.

First, each person added *within* the care team creates additional coordination challenges. Communication among members of a healthcare team, especially members with different background training and unique professional languages, can be challenging. Across many practice types, physicians tend to work independently, frequently moving from a clinic setting to a hospital setting, and sometimes a surgical setting as well. At each location, the additional care team members work to coordinate an intersection between a physician and his/her patients. Meanwhile, each setting typically has its own communication style, workflow, and "workarounds." This can make it difficult for physicians to move from one care team to another, without truly knowing the inner workings of any particular team. It is difficult too for care teams to welcome rotating physicians one after the other, each with their own idiosyncrasies.

Second, shared decision-making and motivational interviewing frequently lead to referrals requiring handoffs *between* care teams. A handoff is the transfer of information about a patient, along with professional responsibility and accountability for the patient. As health care has become more complex, handoffs have become much more frequent without a standardized way to conduct them. This makes handoffs a vulnerable time for patients, and if done poorly, they can worsen outcomes and raise the costs of care (i.e., decrease value).

Third, and perhaps most important given the hierarchical nature of healthcare delivery, a disengaged physician can sabotage all the efforts of the other team members. Simply put, physicians are the leaders of care teams. As such, their actions send signals to patients and other team members. If a physician does not acknowledge the work done by patients to complete patient-reported measures or does not take visible action based on the measures, patients and team members will begin to question their value in the treatment plan. If a physician casually passes out patient decision support tools as though they were merely parting gifts, patients will not use them, and team members will lose interest in learning how the process of shared decision-making can increase the value of the care being delivered.

It is for these reasons that physicians must lead the way in demonstrating how to use patient-reported measures at the point of care and use the OODA (observe, orient, decide, act) loop to help improve outcomes and decrease costs. *Observing* and reviewing patient-reported measures can more efficiently *orient* the necessary team members to address what matters most to the current patient as well as inform patients about average outcomes for similar patients choosing each of the available options. Physicians must demonstrate a willingness to work with team members to build shared language and shared knowledge about the techniques and tools that can support the *decision*-making process. And it is physicians who must be facile enough with motivational interviewing techniques to support the care team's efforts to overcome ambivalence and build confidence in patients needing to take new *actions*.

9.2 Conclusion

The OODA loop approach, PROMs at the point of care, shared decision-making, and motivational interviewing are not meant to be tricks we use to "guide" patients toward the behavior and outcomes that matter to us. Rather, these tools help us find what matters most to patients.

As providers, on our best days, we are all capable of finding what matters to patients and communicating clearly them. We should strive to do this with every patient every time, not because it may save some poorly defined amount of money for our country, hospital, or clinic, or because we might be financially rewarded for doing so. Rather, we strive because it creates the type of care we would want for our own aging parents, our spouse with a chronic condition, or our sick child. These tools help us stay aligned with our core values on the days we may not be at our best, when we are rushed, stressed, and tired. After all, if we only take up the tools that help us better care for our patients when there are promises for higher payment or threats of financial punishment if we do not, then we are only responding to carrots and sticks—we would be managed, rather than being stewards of healthcare professions.

Bibliography

Durand, M. A., P. J. Barr, T. Walsh, et al. (2014). Incentiving shared decision-making in the USA – Where are we now? *Healthcare* 3, no.2:97–101. doi:10.1016/j.hjdsi.2014.10.008.

Nelson, W. A., E. Taylor, and T. Walsh. (2014). Leadership and transition: Building an ethical organizational culture. *The Health Care Manager* 33, no. 3:158–164.

Nelson, W. A. and T. Walsh. (2014). Ensuring patient-centered care. *The Healthcare Executive* 29, no. 4:40–42.

Walsh, T., P. J. Barr, R. Thompson, et al. (2014). Undetermined impact of patient decision support interventions on health care costs and savings. *BMJ* 348:g188. doi:10.1136/bmj.g188.

Westling, C., T. Walsh, and W. A. Nelson. (2017). Perceived ethics dilemmas among pioneer accountable care organizations. *Journal of Healthcare Management* 62, no. 1:18–27.

Chapter 10

Subject matter expert interviews

The first nine chapters of this book put together all of the elements of getting to what matters most to patients. There is a lot to absorb there, and you can see that there is a great deal of work ahead of anyone who plans to embark on such an endeavor. But you want to know how the elements and tools are put into practice across an enterprise. You probably also want to know what some of the challenges and potential rewards are, and why professionals who have made these strides believe they have been worth the effort.

Because experience is the best teacher, the last and longest chapter of the book is devoted to interviews with nine subject matter experts who have diverse backgrounds in implementing many of the tools and processes presented in this book. In these interactions, they share how they became interested in patient-reported outcomes and shared decision-making. They provide insight into how they got over significant organizational and operational barriers to implementation and created an environment that encouraged people to embrace change.

10.1 Kevin Bozic, MD

Bio

Kevin Bozic is the inaugural Chair of Surgery and Perioperative Care at the Dell Medical School at UT Austin. He is a nationally recognized leader in orthopedic surgery and value-based healthcare payment and delivery models. Prior to joining the Dell Medical School, he was the William R. Murray Endowed Professor and Vice Chair of Orthopedic Surgery at the University of California San Francisco (UCSF) School of Medicine, and Core Faculty of the Philip R. Lee Institute for Health Policy Studies. He holds a Bachelor of Science degree in Biomedical Engineering from Duke University, and an MD with Thesis degree from UCSF. He completed his Orthopedic Surgery Residency training in the Harvard Combined Orthopedic Residency Program, and additional Fellowship training in Adult Reconstructive Surgery from Rush University Medical Center in Chicago. Dr. Bozic also holds a master's degree in business administration from Harvard Business School (HBS), where he continues to serve as a Senior Institute Associate in Professor Michael Porter's Institute for Strategy and Competitiveness.

Dr. Bozic has extensive research and policy experience in the growing field of value-based health care with a focus on the implementation and evaluation of value-based payment and delivery models. Dr. Bozic is also actively involved in numerous regional and national health policy initiatives, including the American Joint Replacement Registry Steering Committee (as Chair), the Yale Center for Outcomes Research & Evaluation (CORE) Performance Measurement Group, the Institute for Healthcare Improvement, and the Joint Commission Technical Advisory Panel. He is the co-founder and former Chair of the California Joint Replacement Registry, past Chair of the American Academy of Orthopedic Surgeons Council on Research and Quality, and a former member of the Agency for Health Care Research & Quality Effective Health Care Stakeholder Group.

How did you become interested in patient-reported outcomes and shared decision-making?

Well, as an orthopedic surgeon, I realized early on that our treatments and interventions are designed to improve function and quality of life, and reduce pain. They really don't have any other intent. They're not intended to extend life, nor are they intended to cure any sort of disease. And so ultimately, the only goals we have are to reduce pain and improve function. And so it became obvious that we needed tools to measure how well we were meeting those goals. Fortunately, there were many tools that had been well researched but, unfortunately, not many had been used routinely in a clinical setting.

It was also very obvious that the conditions we treat are what I would consider preference-sensitive conditions. Among orthopedic conditions, which by definition are preference-sensitive conditions, there's rarely a single "right answer" in terms of treatment, so the most effective way to determine appropriate treatment is to engage the patient in a shared decision-making conversation. In doing so, I also realized that patients don't have our fund of knowledge regarding the pathophysiology of disease and the treatment alternatives. And we don't have our patient's fund of knowledge when it comes to their preferences and values and the reasons for seeking treatment in the first place. So I found the shared decision-making framework to be a very effective tool for efficiently combining a provider's extensive knowledge of pathophysiology of the disease and treatment options with a patient's knowledge of their preferences, values, and goals of treatment.

Could you say more about how you're using these tools currently in your setting with patients?

The first thing we do before they come to see us—preferably a day or two prior, but no later than the day they arrive and before they meet with the provider—is we get a baseline assessment of their physical and mental health, their level of activation, and their thinking about their involvement in managing their own health. We take that information and put it into a predictive analytic tool that tells us—based on the individual's self-reported pain, function, physical health, and mental health—their likelihood of achieving their goals with a variety of different treatment alternatives, both surgical and non-surgical. And then we use that information in a structured shared decision-making conversation with the patient about what they feel would be the most appropriate treatment for their condition.

Just to be clear, the innovation that you created with this shared decision-making process has been to make it highly personalized. You're taking that patient's scores and letting him/her know what treatment in your facility is likely to do for him/her based on where he/she is starting from and all the other patients that you've seen.

Exactly right. Rather than using off-the-shelf decision aids, which provide some useful information about pathophysiology of disease and the treatment options that are based on large studies of relatively homogenous populations providing an average likelihood of achieving a positive or negative outcome, our approach tries to get a much more customized assessment that's based on that patient's own clinical and demographic characteristics, and physical and mental health.

There's an Amazon-like quality to what you're describing: "If you read this book, and from all we know about other people that have read that book, you might enjoy this other book." So you're able to say to a patient, given the array of scores you've provided, and all the other patients' scores we've collected, these are the likely outcomes for you.

That's correct.

How did you get your organization to this point?
The first thing was to convince the providers, the administrative team, and most importantly, the patients, of the value of this kind of information. I think that it's not commonly used in healthcare and I think that patients and providers see it as a "nice-to-have," not a "need-to-have."

The next barriers are logistical and operational: How will we get the information in the right place to the patients and the providers in real time, when they need it so that it's not being looked at in retrospect?

Then finally, the business model remains a potential barrier for incorporating this type of decision-making.

Given these barriers, how did you create an environment where people were willing to make that change?
I learned that it starts from the top. You have to have buy-in from the leaders of the organization that this is a must-have, not a nice-to-have. So it begins by building shared language and shared knowledge among the organizational leadership and building commitment from the top that we will assess outcomes from the patient's perspective for every patient.

I think at that point, then other people in the organization start to believe this must be important. And then they start to ask, "How I can use this information to my advantage?" And so practitioners then wanted more education regarding how to use the information. How do you have conversations with patients about the information? How can it be helpful to you in selecting and discussing treatment options with patients?

And then with patients, we found what's most important is making sure that it's discussed every visit with every patient, because if it's not, it just seems like another form or another survey that they're asked to fill out. They believe it didn't really impact their care and they have no shortage of wasteful forms to fill out when they visit a healthcare provider.

How did you address the operational challenges?

We tried to identify a vendor that could capture this information in the electronic health records (EHR) seamlessly, like a lab value, but we learned there were not any EHRs that had prioritized integrating patient-reported outcomes. The patient portals and other interfaces are generally not user friendly enough to make them useful for, or practical for, patients. Then, through trial and error and keeping an emphasis on critical information, we started making a big push to gather the data when patients book appointments. If we're not able to do it then, we want to do it when they check in. We hand them an iPad and get the information then and then have a real-time connection to the EHR, so as soon as that patient completes his or her survey, it's scored and it's available in the EHR. Then the provider team can view it. I would not say we have this completely figured out, but again, we're committed to finding solutions and constantly iterating to improve because it's a priority for our organization.

How about the financial barrier? In a fee-for-service environment, there's a theory that using patient-reported information and a shared decision-making process may lead to a decrease in the utilization of invasive procedures. Have you seen that or how did you deal with that worry?

In our model, we are working to change the incentive system so that the incentives are around optimizing the health of the patients and minimizing the total episode costs. To do this we've pushed hard for a number of condition-based bundled payments where we're paid for the management of the condition rather than for the procedure. And so actually the margins for us are higher when we're paid at the condition level than at the procedure level. We're incentivized to provide the right care for that patient that's going to help us achieve the optimal outcome. We know for instance that for a patient with severe anxiety or depression, even if they have advanced pathophysiology in their musculoskeletal disease, it's unlikely that surgery right then is going to benefit that patient. So, if our incentives are truly based on improving health and in controlling cost, it makes sense to address the mood disorder and then, if needed, revisit the surgical treatment option.

The other way I explain this to other physicians who are not in that type of environment is none of us like unhappy patients. So all of us would love to have strategies to identify ahead of time who is least likely to benefit from a surgical intervention and be able to identify and treat them through another path rather than find out later that surgery was probably a bad choice for that patient because they had a low likelihood of achieving their outcome and a high likelihood of being dissatisfied. I believe having patient-reported measures at the point of care and a shared decision-making process helps decrease the likelihood of a patient being dissatisfied. One thing I've found most helpful now is having this data and being able to share it with patients makes conversations much easier. Rather than saying—"I just don't think you're quite right for surgery; I can't put my finger on it but there's something about you that makes me nervous."— now I can say, "Look, based on your own data, your likelihood of achieving your goals through treatment '1' is 'X' and with treatment '2' it is 'Y'" and then having a conversation where they come to that conclusion. I've found that being armed with that data it makes for a much more effective and productive conversation.

Once you've grasped the conversational aspect of it, your efficiency and your effectiveness with patients improves. So rather than being an additional burden, the data are helpful. I think that's underappreciated.

Regarding the worry about less utilization of invasive procedures, I'm still eager to see a rigorous study with good data on utilization rates before starting shared decision-making and then following those rates over a long period of time, a minimum of five years. This is important because patients may delay a procedure, particularly an orthopedic procedure. Prior research that found less utilization of certain procedures following shared decision-making used shorter time horizons, say, one year or even just a six-month period. So, it's important for people to understand that the worry about lower utilization has been mostly theoretically or observed in short-term studies. The longer term effects have not been empirically determined.

And beyond utilization rates, if a patient comes to see me and he/she has predictors of a negative outcome but I miss them and operate anyway, that patient may now be destined to a lifetime of misery, and that likely makes their provider miserable as well. If we use the data to build trust with patients and optimize risk factors such as untreated anxiety and depression, and delay that procedure, they may have more realistic expectations and a better psychological milieu and greater resiliency. It is then more likely that patient will have a good outcome and then be less reliant on the health system going forward.

Any additional advice you have for a place that's interested in getting started?
I just want to reemphasize how the payment model really does influence the likelihood of adopting this type of approach. It you're in any sort of a value-based payment model, particularly condition-based bundled payments, it really does make these types of tools essential. They become your business intelligence.

Also, I can't emphasize enough how important it is to be discussing these results with patients and explaining that it's their perspective that matters because patients are not used to any of this. It's not the paradigm that they're used to, so they can be just as resistant as providers until you actually start using the information in the clinic.

Finally, I'll just say that anyone that I know that began measuring outcomes from the patient's perspective and incorporating that into shared decision-making conversations just finds their overall practice to be more rewarding and fulfilling. I think this is because they're now focused on the things that really matter to the patient. I don't know any providers that don't ultimately want to improve the health of the people they have the privilege of treating. These tools make that a more effective and efficient process, but also give you a better sense of whether or not you're achieving your goals. They give you the feedback you need to understand whether the treatment you are providing actually improves a patient's health from their own perspective.

10.2 Ted Rooney RN, MPH

Bio

Ted Rooney combines his vocation and avocation for health care in semi-retirement by volunteering and working in Maine with the Maine Council on Aging and Maine Quality Counts, helping to better connect healthcare and social service providers in service of older adults. Maine's older adults want healthcare and social service providers to help them live active and healthy lives in their homes and communities, and focus on the goals important to them.

Formerly, Ted was Project Leader for Aligning Forces for Quality from 2007 to 2015, a Robert Wood Johnson Foundation funded initiative led in Maine by Quality Counts in partnership with the Maine Quality Forum and Maine Health Management Coalition. He also led the Maine Health Management Coalition's Pathways to Excellence initiatives from 2002 to 2014, which measured and reported the value of health care, and worked to change the reimbursement system to reward high-value care. As part of that work, Ted facilitated labor-management groups working together to purchase high-value health care. Before that Ted was project manager for a three-year ergonomics study looking at the effect of ergonomic chairs on the health outcomes and productivity of employees. Previously, Ted managed population health programs for L.L. Bean for 15 years, where he also served as a beta-site director for the development of patient-reported outcome instruments. He has undergraduate degrees in sociology and nursing, and a master's degree in public health.

Please describe the link you see between patient-reported outcome measures and outcomes that matter to patients.

We know only about 20% of "health" comes from medical care, and most of us know that health is simply a means to an end, which is a joyful life. For example, in my current work with aging populations, we know 90% of seniors want to stay in their homes and communities as long as possible. Yet that is not what is being measured. Throughout most of the history of healthcare measurement, the conceptual model has been on Donebedian's model of structure, process, and outcomes with the focus on structure and process. In theory, this meant building healthcare delivery systems that had the right people in the right place doing the right thing. By this I mean first assuring educated, licensed, and certified individuals are providing care, and then asking, "Are those people following evidence-based guidelines?" In these areas, we have made real progress in the last few decades. Clinical outcomes have been much harder, but here too we are making progress. What proportion of your patients has an A1C level above nine? What proportion of your patients has their blood pressure well-controlled? We're getting there. It was just 10 to 15 years ago when process guidelines were considered heresy—"cookbook" medicine. But there still is a gulf between the clinical process measures and clinical outcome measures and what patients actually want out of health care, which is a more productive and meaningful life. Even employers, who pay most healthcare expenses, want productive, healthy employees, which are connected to but different from measures of gym attendance, body mass, or blood pressure, for instance.

I can empathize with providers who are highly educated, competitive, and want to do the right thing, but who get flummoxed when all of a sudden they're going to be held responsible for something the patient does, and those actions by the patient seem like they are out of their control. A sense of fairness and concern arises.

Interestingly, I've spent a lot of time talking with physicians over the years. What one physician might see as patient behavior out of their control, another physician sees as a need for motivational interviewing and a team with a social worker and health coach to help the patient with the myriad challenges that may be getting in the way of adherence. Some members of the team are just better able to connect with different patients. For this reason, outcomes of care may well be more appropriate at the provider team level.

So, we're getting there and there's a confluence of a number of different events coming together that I think gives us a real opportunity now to begin to really measure things that matter to patients and then link that to healthcare delivery. The biggest driver is the move toward payment models that consider outcomes that matter. And it is happening. The Centers for Medicare and Medicaid Services has a webpage on "measures that matter." I really think payment changes will be the ultimate driver because the status quo culture is so strong in health care.

What challenges do you see to wider adoption of patient-reported outcome measures?
I continually hear doctors call patient-reported outcome measures and patient experience measures "patient satisfaction surveys." This is a mistake. Questions like, "How has your mood been over the past week?" or "Were you treated with

respect by the providers?" or "Did you understand the instructions you were given?" are distinct from satisfaction, and patients understand they are distinct.

I think we also need to get to the point where information from the patient about what matters most to them is available and used during his or her visit with a provider. So, an individual patient's information is used immediately to influence, and hopefully improve, the care of that patient. The information can become part of the medical record later and it can be aggregated for process improvement efforts or reimbursement later. When the measures are not used at the point of care, patients and providers can see them as a burden, something just for research, or worst of all, a simplistic and incomplete way to grade providers.

I also think we need to find ways to keep someone who does not have health issues from going through 20 questions. Patients can respond to the first couple of questions, and their answers tell us we do or do not need to keep going down this road or we do have enough information to stop. This dynamic modeling respects patients' time but it also helps providers. Adaptive questioning can keep us from just flooding the providers with more and more data that need attention.

This isn't very different from what we do now with cholesterol issues. I may have a blood test and a phone call or email with my provider. Or I may have the test and then an in-person visit, but the blood test always comes first, so when I sit down with my provider they have my results. We need to get people to think of patient-reported measures like they do the clinical variables.

This also brings up the need to think about how we collect, organize, and display information. We can learn from fighter pilots where a lot of time has been spent deciphering what information they do need, when do they need it, and how can we display it so they can't miss it. We need something like that in health care.

What recommendations do you have for providers just starting to use patient-reported outcome measures?

I'm a fan of trying the smallest possible step when changing workflow, so if I was just starting to use patient-reported measures today, I'd probably start with something like the PHQ depression measures, because that's currently one of the measures in alternative payment models. It's a depression screening (PHQ-2) and measurement (PHQ-9) tool. This is important because many of our patients who utilize a lot of health care have comorbid mood disorders and, if left unaddressed, this affects their ability to care for themselves. The PHQ-2 is a sensitive screening tool to identify patients at risk, and the PHQ-9 is a good measurement tool to help diagnose depression and monitor whether it improves or not. Therefore, you could use the tools to help funnel patients toward selective serotonin reuptake inhibitors (SSRI) and/or counseling or working with an integrated team. I think that's an ideal way to go. Moreover, there are protocols out there showing how providers can improve their care processes. It might sound simple, but it is not. The survey needs to be looked at and discussed with the patient. Then there may need to be a warm hand-off to somebody who knows cognitive behavioral therapy techniques, motivational interviewing, etc. Providers worry they'll have to bear the burden of talking with patients about their depression during a busy, hectic schedule, but it doesn't have to be like that with a team-based approach.

Primary care is an obvious place to start and I think orthopedics is also prime because orthopedic problems are seldom fatal, can last a long time, and have a big impact on a person's perception of their health and well-being. And the orthopedist societies are pushing outcome measures for all these reasons.

How do you see patient-reported outcome measures being used in the future?

In the future, we'll have more and more baby boomers retiring with multiple chronic illnesses where we'll need to keep track of everybody and how they're doing from year to year. I can imagine coming into my annual wellness visit and my hope would be that as I enter the provider's office, the team there has a summary of what matters most to me and a comparison of my last couple of years as a trend analysis. You can imagine smart software alerting them to which of my areas need further probing and then they can immediately sit down with me and say, "We see that has changed," so it's an entree into a dialogue around things that are important to me. And we don't have to spend most of the visit getting there.

There are a couple of ways I think the collection of patient-reported outcomes can really help a practice. First, I think if there's any competitive market where someone's trying to get employer accounts, which are usually the better paying ones, the practice that can show that it's actually delivering improved outcomes will win out. And there's a first mover advantage here! Simply demonstrating your ability to collect outcomes and having a willingness to share plans to improve them, neither of which requires sharing actual scores, can sometimes justify a higher fee schedule. That is a marketing approach for anybody who wants to get business with employers.

Second, I've seen how the use of these measures helps providers to practice clinical care with their hearts. They begin to see these outcomes not just as an arbitrary imposition to measure their quality, and come to appreciate how these tools give insight into what is really important to their patients. In fact, and this amazes me, almost all care providers already ask one or more questions from an outcome survey sometime during the day. They ask, "How are you doing?" or "Were you able to do your yard work?" but they rarely stop and quantify the answers in a way that allows them to begin to understand just how important these "conversation making" questions are to patients, or how they are trending over time. These questions are how to connect with patients and the connection is how patients feel listened to and understood. In short, they matter! The use of surveys can help to launch these conversations, quantify progress, and learn from trends. Having conversations with patients about what is important to them, and seeing them grow and get better over time gets you up in the morning wanting to practice medicine! So, I'm bullish if we can get a heart-focused approach to supporting outcomes among providers and at the same time get payment reform financially rewarding improvements in patient outcomes, the goals important to them, and their overall quality of life. That's the head part, the business of health care. I think combining the heart and the head is the sweet spot.

10.3 Libby Hoy, Founder/CEO patient- and family-centered care partners

Bio

As the mother of three sons living with mitochondrial disease, Libby Hoy has 20 years of experience navigating the healthcare system. She began volunteering as a parent mentor in 1995 and has been working to improve health systems and empower patients and families to be active partners in care ever since. In her role as the first Family Advocate at Miller Children's Hospital, she developed the Parent Advisory Board and created the structure for the long-term integration of the patient and family voice within the organization. Libby has presented at multiple national and international conferences on subjects related to patient-and family-centered care (PFCC) practice. As a consultant, Libby strives to share the evidence, practices, and methods that support PFCC culture in healthcare organizations.

In 2010, Libby founded PFCC partners to create a community of patients, families, providers, and healthcare organizations committed to the shared learning of patient-and family-centered care practice. PFCC Partners also established the PFA Network, inclusive of more than 150 Patient Family Advisors working in healthcare settings across the country to collaborate for improvement in the quality, safety, experience, and delivery of health care.

Libby has served as an advisor to Patient Centered Outcomes Research Institute (PCORI), Partnership for Patients, Institute of Medicine (IOM), National Quality Forum (NQF), and as faculty for the Institute for Healthcare Improvement (IHI). In these and all efforts, Libby strives to build the infrastructure and capacity for healthcare organizations to engage all patients and families, from the bedside to the boardroom.

How did you become interested in shared decision-making and how do you see it being used in healthcare delivery today?

I was introduced early to the concept of active participation in the care of my three sons. In the ensuing 25 years of experience as a caregiver and patient in the healthcare system, I witnessed a slow trend from "informed consent" to the evolution we call shared decision-making. The concept of shared decision-making (SDM) is still evolving from a time when the decision of the doctor was shared with the patient. (Believe it or not, when we started out, even the decisions made for the patient was not shared with the patient.) True shared decision-making is a communication strategy—a relationship foundation. It requires three components, as defined by the National Quality Forum. First, clinicians need to share information in a way that can be understood for all evidence-based options, including the option to do nothing. Second, clinicians tailor information for the individual patient. And third, the patient's values and priorities inform the decision making process. In today's interactions with clinicians' I think we are still somewhat confusing SDM with decision making aids. The former is a way of communicating. The latter is a tool that supports that communication.

Describe how you see the link between SDM and outcomes that matter to patients.

Patients who have the opportunity to be active participants in the decision-making process, or the clinician encounter more broadly, seem to be more invested in the decision because their needs and priorities are reflected in it. Take for example a conversation my son had with his doctor about whether or not he could go snowboarding with a peripherally inserted central catheter. As they talked through the risks and his desire to be a "normal" 16-year-old, each worked through the various risks, likely outcomes, and advantages. When they settled on the conditions under which he could snowboard, he was fully invested in taking those precautions because he was part of identifying what those precautions would be and he understood fully why they were important. Imagine a scenario where he did not have that level of communication with his physician. Telling a vulnerable 16-yearold living with chronic illness he couldn't go snowboarding without discussion would disempower him, in the moment and in the relationship going forward. The clinician can them become an adversary, especially to a teenage boy. The opportunity is not for patients to get everything they want, it is the opportunity for the patient to truly be part of the team and have the ability to fully impact his or her own outcomes.

Describe challenges to the wider adoption of SDM that you've experienced or witnessed.

I'm excited about the opportunity SDM is bringing to people experiencing illness. The potential to empower people to be active in their health and health care is tremendous. One of the biggest challenges I see in its current evolution is the need to shift the public's perspective of their role in health care. Much effort is taking place to raise the capacity of the clinical workforce to participate fully in SDM; however, little attention is going toward educating the public about the opportunity they have to participate in this way. If our clinical staff is ready and prepared but does not encounter patients who are aware of the opportunity to participate in this way and have their priorities inform care, it's highly likely the opportunity for SDM will be missed.

What recommendations do you have for healthcare delivery systems beginning to use these tools and techniques?

Engage your patients and family caregivers. I tend to think that's the right answer for most every issue in health care, but even more so when it comes to SDM. Involving patient family populations will help local clinicians understand how their patient population can best participate in SDM efforts. They can review SDM tools for effectiveness and help to design and evaluate SDM programs. An evaluation of SDM that does not take into account the patient's perspective only serves half of the team. Since SDM is a communication strategy between two humans, it doesn't make sense to only learn from half the team.

What future role/vision do you have in this area and what drives that vision?

As the nurturer of the Patient Family Advisor Network (www. pfanetwork.org), I have a responsibility to raise the capacity of the 600+ advisors in the network to begin the SDM conversation with their organizations and to become passionate disseminators of best SDM practices. Finally, through that network and our activities, we work to identify ways to promote a shift in the public expectations of their role in their health and healthcare.

What barriers (e.g., organizational, policy, education, training for med students and existing providers, etc.) do you see to the implementation of that vision, and what is needed to overcome them?

There is a fair amount of good work under way to address medical education in SDM and we will certainly continue to support those. More work is needed at the policy level to make SDM a standard of care. Many suggest an analysis of SDM's ROI may be helpful in nudging health system leaders toward implementation, and an incentive structure from CMS could also drive change. In terms of shifting public opinion, I think we may see early adopters promoting SDM as a market distinguisher that may drive the shift in public perception. As a patient-driven organization, we will certainly keep driving that message as well.

10.4 William Kramer

Bio
Bill Kramer is Executive Director for Health Policy at the Pacific Business Group on Health. Bill is also Project Director for the Consumer-Purchaser Alliance, an initiative to improve the quality and affordability of health care. Bill serves on the National Quality Forum's Board of Directors, the Patient Center Primary Care Collaborative's Board, and the NQF's Measure Applications Partnership Coordinating Committee. Immediately before taking his position at PBGH, Bill led his own consulting practice focusing on health reform, finance, and business strategy for public and private sector clients. Prior to developing his consulting practice, Bill was a senior executive with Kaiser Permanente for over 20 years—most recently as Chief Financial Officer for Kaiser Permanente's Northwest Region. Bill also served as general manager for Kaiser Permanente's operations in Connecticut; earlier in his career, he managed marketing, human resources, and medical economics functions. Bill has an MBA from the Stanford Graduate School of Business and a BA from Harvard.

How do you see the link between PROMs and outcomes that matter to patients?
Patient-reported outcomes measures are the best way to measure whether a patient's health has improved following a procedure or treatment regimen. PROMs—unlike traditional clinical outcomes—are framed in the way that patients talk about the healthcare services they've received. When I tore my ACL playing basketball and went in for ACL-replacement surgery, my biggest question was how soon I could get back on the basketball court. The surgeon (who was very skilled, I

believe) was more concerned about whether the procedure was done "right" and that no infection occurred. I know that these traditional clinical measures are important, and I assume the doctor and hospital are watching them, but they didn't give me a full picture about whether my surgery was "successful." Patients want to know whether they will be healthier and be able to resume their normal activities, and that information can be captured only through PROMs.

Describe challenges to the wider adoption of PROs that you've experienced or witnessed.

There are real obstacles to the wider adoption of PROs, based on what I have observed at PBGH and my work on the NQF Board. For example, there are administrative costs involved in the collection of PROs for healthcare systems and providers, and there are difficulties getting a high response rate from patients. There is a lack of standardization across PRO measures and PRO collection tools; as a result, it's difficult for consumers to compare providers on these measures. The integration of PRO data into electronic health records remains a challenge. The mechanics of integration are not difficult; it's not a technological problem. It is a problem of will. When purchasers and consumers recognize the value of PROMs and begin to insist in their widespread use, and when providers realize how valuable they are for patient care, we will be able to overcome the technical and administrative obstacle.

What advice do you have for delivery systems that have begun using these tools and seek to maximize their effect on outcomes that matter and/or the costs of delivering care?

It is important to first find a way to integrate PROMs data with clinical outcomes data in electronic health records. That enables the reengineering of clinical workflows to make best use of PROMs data. For example, the clinician should be able to review the data in advance of and during a patient's office visit (or virtual encounter) and use it to inform the treatment plan and discussion with the patient. Working upstream, a goal-setting process must be incorporated via dialogue between the clinician team and the patient. The goals should provide the basis for the interpretation of subsequent PROM data, i.e., to what extent is the patient's health/functional status meeting or exceeding the goals. And remember, there is no need to recreate the wheel. Use standardized PROM tools and data capture protocols that are consistent with those used by other providers; this enables benchmarking and appropriate comparisons.

What future role/vision do you have in this area and what drives that vision?

In the future, I believe PROMs and clinical outcomes measures will be standardized and used by all providers, and they will gradually supplant the process and structure measures that have historically dominated quality reporting. Those traditional measures may not go away, rather the patients' perspective will be routinely incorporated and valued.

The standardized PROMs and clinical outcomes will be publicly reported and used by patients as the primary tool for selecting providers and treatments, and PROMs data will be used by clinicians as an essential element in treatment planning and patient care. Patients will see the value of the measures for capturing their voice and for deciding among treatment options. Providers will see how the use of PROMs in planning and at the point of care can help improve the effectiveness and efficiency of treatments and clinical encounters.

I also believe PROMs will be widely used by health systems to identify best practices and quality improvement initiatives.

What barriers (e.g., organizational, policy, education, training for med students and existing providers, etc.) do you see to the implementation of that vision, and what is needed to overcome them?

Clinicians need to embrace the use of PROMs data as an essential element of patient care. I believe the ability to use these data will be an important aspect to this acceptance. It is revelatory once a clinician understands how the data from a patient can augment their understanding of *that patient during care planning and encounters.*

To get there, provider groups and health systems need to invest in PROMs data collection and integration into electronic health records. At that point, we'll need to establish and enforce an expectation that standardized PROM tools and PROMs will be collected and reported by all providers.

Finally, private health plans and public payers need to set expectations that PROMs will be collected, publicly reported, and used in value-based payment arrangements.

10.5 Carla Marienfeld, MD

Bio
Carla Marienfeld is the co-author of "Motivational Interviewing for Clinical Practice" and an Associate Professor of Psychiatry at University of California, San Diego. Clinically, she focuses on the treatment of patients with substance-use disorders and comorbid psychiatric conditions. Her academic interests focus on implementation research and large-data health outcomes for patients with substance-use disorders. She attended Baylor College of Medicine in Houston, Texas, where she completed the International Health Track, and earned Alpha Omega Alpha (AOA) Medical Honors Society distinction. During psychiatry residency at Yale, she served as chief resident. She completed a fellowship in addiction psychiatry at Yale, and she founded and led the Yale Global Mental Health Program. She is the Director of Addiction Services for University of California, San Diego, and the Medical Director of the UCSD Addiction Recovery and Treatment Program in La Jolla, California.

How did you become interested in Motivational Interviewing (MI)?
I was exposed to some of the core ideas through various curricula in medical school under many different names,

including patient-centered interviewing, and other modalities. It always made sense to me, and I think I was fortunate to have good role models so that I could see what it looked like in practice. This is key—much better than just agreeing with something in principle, but not understanding how to do it in the real world. My biggest exposure came from learning about motivational interviewing during my addiction psychiatry fellowship. A mentor had a grant that allowed for us to have a two-day intensive training, followed by weekly supervision and scoring of recorded sessions with patients. The name "motivational interviewing" is a bit misleading, since it's not really an interview in the traditional sense. But, it is based on mutual respect and eliciting from the patient what they want to do based on their values and goals. I think of myself in the role of facilitator, and this is an enjoyable way to help patients in their recovery. I am also interested in not burning out after seeing sometimes 20 patients a day. MI is a way to participate with the patient rather than having the patient work against you.

Describe how you see the link between MI and outcomes that matter to patients.
I am often surprised at what the priorities are for patients. The outcomes they seek are sometimes what I might guess and sometimes not. The beauty of MI is that I don't have to guess. In addition, once I know what matters to the patient, I can work with the patient to achieve that outcome. I may also have goals or recommendations for the patient as well, but through the process of MI, any positive change gets things moving in the right direction.

Describe challenges to the wider adoption of MI that you've experienced or witnessed.
The ideas of MI are easy to understand. However, just like in the behaviors we are asking patients to change, changing our own behavior takes time and practice. It's challenging to find ongoing mentorship and supervision to continue to practice

MI in many clinical settings. There are networks and training programs that build this in, but for the average person who attends a few-hour training, it may not be enough. Without practice, feedback, and refinement, our tendency is to go back to what we've always done.

A common misconception I see is the concern that patients may prefer an outcome that is not rationale. Patients may not always know what they want or how to get there, but once we find something, it's always something I can get behind. I have yet to have a patient seriously tell me that they want an outcome that is harmful to them. If a patient is suicidal or at risk for harming themselves, then safety always becomes the priority, but through MI, when you have engaged a patient, we can usually find something that we can agree is a positive step.

What recommendations do you have for healthcare delivery systems beginning to use these tools and techniques?

I'd recommend learning more about implementation science and what we know about changing behavior. Both have a lot to offer. The most helpful things an organization can do include providing space to create new processes, knowledge to do them, support to implement and refine them, and the follow-up to continue doing them. It's not a one-and-done thing—not with helping patients and not with changing health systems.

There are online resources created to help providers learn and refine motivational interviewing skills and to help systems disseminate concepts, implement innovative approaches, and learn over time. Visit the sites below to learn more.

■ The Motivational Interviewing Network of Trainers (http://www.motivationalinterviewing.org/about_mint)
■ Brief Action Planning (https://centrecmi.ca/brief-action-planning/)
■ The Center on Alcoholism, Substance Abuse, & Addictions (https://casaa.unm.edu/mimanuals.html)

What future role/vision do you have in this area and what drives that vision?

I would like to continue building training opportunities and ongoing support to help others try this approach. This is also my own form of constantly learning and relearning the technique, practicing it, and improving it so that I can continue to use it effectively.

What barriers do you see to the implementation of that vision, and what is needed to overcome them?

The same barriers that we have in changing most behaviors. We need the time and space to make the change, consistency in our approach (practice and refinement), supervision (feedback to continue to improve), and ways to manage competing interests (other skills, knowledge needed, system needs).

10.6 Matt Handley, MD

Bio

Matt Handley is the Senior Associate Medical Director for Quality and Safety for Kaiser Permanente of Washington. He maintains a primary care practice in Seattle. He leads work to improve patient safety and traditional clinical quality and quality improvement strategies. He also leads work to improve clinical value/resource stewardship, leading work in shared decision-making, reducing unintended clinical variation, and reducing waste. Dr. Handley has participated on the Kaiser National Quality Committee and at the KP Care Management Institute since their inceptions, and is the Permanente Quality Leader leading the work in Life Care Planning across all KP regions.

How did you get started using shared decision-making (SDM)?

During my residency, the first major cardiovascular trials were published, which led to guidelines recommending treatments based on cholesterol. I was fascinated by the recommendations because many of the patients who were recommended treatment were at low overall risk for heart disease and the potential benefit for low-risk patients was surprisingly small. It seemed the expert recommendations were divorced from quantitative information, so I sought to help clinicians and patients to better understand how likely the patient was to benefit from treatment. Over a couple of years, we came up with a way to use the Framingham risk equations and display them in a two-dimensional matrix so that providers and patients could actually understand the likelihood of benefit based on a holistic view of cardiovascular risk.

The most interesting thing was when I had conversations with low-risk patients for whom guidelines recommended treatment, well, very few of those patients were interested in taking the medicine once they understood the benefits and harms of treatment. When patients had more complete knowledge, their values differed from the imputed values that the expert panels assigned to them.

I thought this was very interesting. We then set up a program to train primary care docs to be able to have conversations with patients, again helping them explain the guideline recommendations, the risks, and benefits, and helping them better explain how big (or small) the risks and benefits actually were. The goal was to facilitate a conversation that would uncover how much of a difference matters to the individual who would bear the burden of therapy.

The second story began when prostate cancer screening became popular, around 1991. We recognized the uncertainties were great and the likelihood of benefits seemed likely to be small because of the problem of over diagnosis. So, we set up a similar shared decision-making program where we trained all of our primary care docs in that model of communication. Our use of a shared decision-making model helps the patients in our organization avoid the big spike in diagnosis of prostate cancer that was seen across the country.

In 2008, all kinds of coincidences came together to help us make a much larger investment in SDM. We were lucky to have had many visits from Jack Wennberg, who really helped our leaders understand the opportunity that SDM presented in addressing variation in preference-sensitive care. Many different people helped get the state of Washington to sponsor a collaborative to promote SDM for preference-sensitive surgical conditions. We made the decision to take full advantage of the collaborative and make a large investment in SDM. With some remarkable leadership in our group, we implemented an SDM program for these preference-sensitive conditions. In this work, we targeted treatment choices for spine stenosis, lumbar disc herniation, hip and knee osteoarthritis, early prostate cancer, benign uterine conditions, and breast cancer.

We used classic principles of how to prevent the underuse of effective care that we learned from implementation science. We applied those lessons to build workflows for the reliable distribution of decision aids.

We knew that SDM required more than the use of decision aids—they were necessary, but insufficient to support SDM. We knew we needed our clinicians to have skills in SDM. This led us to launch mandatory training for all of our surgical community. We also made clear our expectations for performance—that we would engage all patients presenting with these diagnoses in SDM, and measure our performance. We were able to get to all of our specialties implemented over about 12 months. Our clinical teams have kept up a high level of performance since that time.

More recently, we've integrated a new tool into our EHR that helps providers communicate likelihood of benefits for patients with cardiovascular disease. The tool pulls discrete data from the EHR that calculates risk and generates pictographs showing the likelihood of different treatments benefiting the patients—a point of care decision aid. It works really well within the timing of an outpatient visit and is very popular with both patients and clinicians.

How do you see the relationship between skills of shared decision-making and finding out what matters most to patients?

I don't think you have SDM without an exploration of a patient's preferences and values. It is the key part of the skill set. I often think the skill set for SDM as including empowering the patient's participation, effective risk communication, and an exploration of what matters to the patient. It takes all three skills to have shared decision-making.

What types of challenges did you run into when you were trying to disseminate the knowledge, skills, and lessons learned across an entire enterprise?

If I've been implying it was easy, well, that's not quite right. This took a lot of concerted work and support over years. Having said that, there are several challenges that I'd like to mention.

The first is really the idea among care providers that, "I already do this." As clinicians, I think we judge ourselves by our intent, which is to provide person-centered care. I think that the vast majority of clinicians are working hard and doing their best based on how they were trained. This often includes the presumption that we already know a patient's preferences. The evidence, however, demonstrates that our ability to implicitly grasp an individual patient's preferences and values is actually quite faulty. Our biggest barrier, then, is that we believe we are better at this than we are.

The second barrier is the belief that all of this is just too complicated. I cannot tell you how many times I hear a provider saying something along the lines of, "I don't even remember the differences in outcomes," which demonstrates that they already know they're not providing full information to their patients about available treatment options.

The third barrier, to me, has to do with risk communication. This is difficult because even when providers "get the numbers right," which isn't easy, their perception of the patient's level of understanding is incorrect. Patients tell us we don't speak in regular English and we talk a thousand words a minute. This is where decision aids are really helpful.

The thing most providers stuck behind these barriers may not fully appreciate; there is a joy in practice that comes from making connections with patients. While there is some upfront time to learn the skills, once learned, you are not slowed down, it is not too complicated, and you can more reliably and consistently make those connections. Connecting on a personal level and helping people is what makes clinical practice so rewarding and interesting. Spend a little more time up front and you will have more joy in practice.

What advice would you have for leaders in an organization just getting starting?
Implementing a program to promote SDM is as much about culture change as it is about the technical change of distribution of decision aids. I see people all the time who try to treat this work as if it is a typical case of underuse, thinking if they can get decision aids delivered like they close care gaps they will be successful. It is really helpful to think about two related but different swim lanes for the work. There is a lane concerned with reliable distribution of decision aids, and an adaptive/cultural the change lane. You want to have conscious efforts to influence the culture as you are working classic clinical improvement strategies. We worked hard to influence clinical opinion leaders so they, in turn, would help us. We also worked to convince senior leaders that this had to be one of the things they routinely talked about and to explain how this makes us a great medical group. This helped with prioritization within the organization, which is always challenging.

What do you see as the future for shared decision-making with patients and how do you see these interactions changing down the road?
I love the quote from the author William Gibson—"the future is already here, it's just not evenly distributed." I think that

there are bright spots, like KP Washington and Dartmouth. I think that there will be innovations in decision aids that make things easier, including making decision aids directly available to patients, which will be helpful. I also look forward to pragmatic tools to help us measure the quality of the conversations to help individual clinicians identify opportunities to improve their skills.

While there will be continued interest in SDM in sophisticated care delivery systems, I think that as we move to value-based payments there will be more interest and investment in SDM.

I think it will take that before we have widespread adoption.

10.7 David Rosengren, MD

Bio

David Rosengren has always been curious about what initiates and sustains motivation and change. This interest began during his early work with angry adolescents and progressed through work in prison, VA and state hospitals, and outpatient settings. His research focus has included addictive behaviors and their sequelae, HIV/AIDS and risk reduction, intimate partner violence, brief interventions, and training methods. Meanwhile, his clinical work extends across a range of treatment populations from those with addictive behaviors to sexual offenders to the chronically mentally ill. Presently, his research evaluates methods for training practitioners and implementation of evidence-based practices.

How did you become interested in motivational interviewing and how do you see it being used in healthcare delivery today?

My interest in patient–provider communication began with shared decision-making and consultant work I did with Bob Pearlman, MD, on end-of-life decisions back in the '90s. His team was creating a workbook to aid people in sorting through these decisions. The workbook was a vehicle to then have discussions with healthcare providers, as well as family members, about end-of-life decisions. Shared decision-making was clearly the appropriate stance for the providers. They had information and resources to share, but this was also a preference-based decision that needed input from the patient and his or her family and as such was one that required a different sort of stance for providers. This was also when I was working with Steve Rollnick on a chapter for *Motivational Interviewing* (MI) (Second Edition) about use of MI within healthcare settings.

Describe how you see the link between MI and outcomes that matter to patients.

This is the crux of the matter. While medicine has developed these powerful interventions, the interplay of patient choices remains central in the outcomes that occur. Smoking and diabetes management are two dramatic examples, but it's evident in most every aspect of medicine where patient actions matter. For patients to act consistently, it has to be something they're invested in, or it simply will not happen. It can still be a challenge when they are invested, but the problem is even bigger when it's our goals and not theirs that take center stage.

Describe challenges to the wider adoption of MI that you've experienced or witnessed.

There are multiple levels of challenge to adoption of MI and it really brings us into the areas of implementation and dissemination science. While of interest to me, these are well beyond the scope of what you're asking for here, but I've experienced all of these challenges. At its most basic, we can look at individual variables for the practitioner (e.g., the degree to which it matches the provider's beliefs, preferences, and skill sets), task variables (e.g., surgery, chemotherapy, weight management), organization variables (e.g., support activities, time allotted, MI champions), and system variables (e.g., reimbursement for which activities). All these contextual elements impede adoption. But, by far the biggest challenge I've experienced is the belief that we can learn a deceptively easy looking skill set in a brief amount of time and that is all the practitioner needs. It is quite clear this skill set needs practice, coaching, and refinement and many individuals and organizations are unwilling to look at these "backend" activities when learning. You can learn the basic ideas of MI over lunch, but you cannot learn to do MI in that amount of time. Its close cousin? "I already do that." Hence, the person doesn't feel they need to learn more. My experience is good MI practitioners never pass up an opportunity to refine skills.

What recommendations do you have for healthcare delivery systems beginning to use these tools and techniques?

Be cognizant of the implementation science literature. This is a growing discipline that provides some clear lines. An excellent 2-day training from a top flight MI trainer is a starting point. If we want the organization to succeed in this effort, and not just sprinkle MI dust on practitioners and hope that magic occurs, we need to commit to the work of learning the practice. The good news is there are a variety of ways to get that done.

What advice do you have for delivery systems that have begun using these tools and seek to maximize their effect on outcomes that matter and/or the costs of delivering care?

Consider a community of practice model where peers meet to discuss techniques, observe samples of each other's practice, and offer feedback. Along these lines, having champions—people in an organization committed to encouraging these steps—is important. It must be champions, because otherwise you're vulnerable to this person leaving or taking a new position and your initiative loses its catalyst. Consistent with this position—and with most any successful initiative—it requires engagement from the organization's leadership.

In terms of cost, there is an issue with billable hours, if you ask a group to do a community of practice. What it does for patients is improve the care they receive and reduce things like failure to comply with medical recommendations, relapses, and return visits. Those are cost and health offsets.

What future role/vision do you have in this area and what drives that vision?

It's an excellent question for which I have no good answer, other than to say my role is minor. However, there are many excellent researchers, writers, and trainers of MI working in this area that are helping to move this idea of shared power and decision-making forward. Twenty-five years ago, when I began this work as an MI trainer in the field of addictions and child welfare, we were heretics. Now MI training is a staple of most graduate schools in the human service fields. Medicine had a little later start, but it's now common for future health-care providers to focus on the quality of the provider–patient interaction, and be intentional in thinking about how decisions are made and implemented.

In terms of my vision, it looks like my endocrinologist, Ken Gross, MD. As a person with Type I diabetes, I see him every three to four months. Whenever he enters the exam room, he sits down and asks me what is going on. It always begins with me and then we go through a shared process of figuring out what needs attention today. I know his time is limited, but he never gives me the impression of being rushed or that we need to move quickly. As a result, the quality of information he gets is better, the solutions fit me, my health behaviors reflect my goals, and the interactions are shorter. My vision is that one day, this is also how my visit with my other docs will go, and no one will even notice, except for maybe some old dogs like me.

What barriers (e.g., organizational, policy, education, training for med students and existing providers, etc.)

do you see to the implementation of that vision, and what is needed to overcome them?

Now, here is the million-dollar question. I believe like most successful implementation efforts, it will require a multilevel and multifocal approach to be successful. Our healthcare system's determination to do things quickly while maximizing revenues leads to a situation that de-emphasizes the patient and emphasizes the provider doing something *to* them. We will need a shift in orientation to a stance of working *with* patients. Much as has happened with complementary and alternative medicine, we'll have to be open to working differently with patients. This is obviously much more of an issue with existing providers where patterns and routines have been set. Within medical school, we may need to reconsider how new providers are trained. There are alternative models, like what Mary Velasquez, Ph.D., is doing with the University of Texas around its medical school training. Providers need technical knowledge, diagnostic skills, sound decision-making, and requisite skills to be successful, all the while embracing this idea that health also requires the active participation of the patient. Lastly, we'll need to take the long view. This is about culture change and that takes time—but it does happen. Don't believe that it can? Just think about what would happen today if you walked into a McDonald's today with a lit cigarette. That's different from what it was 40 years ago.

10.8 Amanda Brownell

Bio

Amanda Brownell is a Licensed Clinical Social Worker and is the Director of Learning and Development at Vital Decisions. She oversees the clinical development of staff that utilizes Motivational Interviewing to empower individuals and their families to engage in advance care planning. The organization's mission is to ensure that all individuals can identify their own values, align them with their end of life choices, and communicate those to their families and medical team. Amanda leads the organization to deliver effective training and coaching to specialists to ensure high-quality interactions with clients. Amanda is a member of the Motivational Interviewing Network of Trainers and is a Designated Association for Talent Development Master Instructional Designer.

Describe how you see the link between Motivational Interviewing (MI) and outcomes that matter to patients.
The techniques utilized in MI are necessary ingredients to understanding and eliciting outcomes that matter most to patients. The use of reflective listening alongside the emphasis on partnership and accurate empathy in MI align with and empower the idea of shared decision-making. They pull down the barriers that exist in the "paternalistic method" where the doctor acts as expert and does not create a space to hear a client's concerns and desires. By using reflective listening and acting as a partner, not an expert, in a client's journey, the health team is able to truly understand what matters most to the patient and help align the treatment options with those values. Once a health team involves a patient as an equal partner in their decisions, they will then truly understand what matters to the client and the patient will be much more likely to follow through on the plan. In turn, the patient's satisfaction with the overall experience also increases.

Describe challenges to the wider adoption of MI that you've experienced
The biggest challenge I've seen to the wider adoption of MI is the lack of investment from the organization/facility in properly training staff in MI. Many organizations bring in trainers in MI for a one- to two-day workshop, but then have no follow-up plan to ensure the techniques transfer to patient care. According to the 70–20–10 model for Learning and

Development, only 10% of learning comes from formal coursework and training. This leaves 90% of the learning to happen from informal learning and on-the-job experiences. For effective job transfer, there needs to be ongoing coaching and support following the formal introductory training. As of yet, few companies are willing to invest in the time or financial cost of this comprehensive training approach. The dissemination of high-quality MI also suffers due to its deceptive simplicity. Organizations or individuals feel they already understand MI and are able to listen effectively. They may use OARS (open-ended questions, affirmations, reflections, and summaries) in their interactions with patients or believe that a little classroom time and a bit of practice is all it takes to use MI. This leads to a lack of importance in committing to ongoing training to further enhance their skills.

What recommendations do you have for healthcare delivery systems beginning to use these tools and techniques?
First, it is imperative for any adult learner to understand what is in it for him or her to learn something new. It will take their time and energy to learn, so each learner needs to feel the new tools and techniques will be beneficial and meaningful to their work. Leaders need to take time to understand what motivates their staff and what will keep them interested in learning this technique. Then, invest time and allocate ongoing resources for staff's understanding and application of MI. It is not enough to simply offer a one- to two-day training. Invest in ongoing coaching support, recordings of their interactions with patients, and time to practice with peers.

What would you recommend for training the staff?
I would recommend a blended learning approach. As mentioned above, having a one- to two-day conceptual training session is only a starting point. Beyond that basic step, it is important to have a plan that involves ongoing coaching, systems of accountability, peer support, and follow-on

trainings. An added bonus would be a forum for employees to learn and reflect at their own pace through self-guided e-learning opportunities.

What future role/vision do you have in this area and what drives that vision?

Understanding outcomes that matter to patients and aligning their care choices with those values is something I am both personally and professionally invested in. Personally, I have witnessed the torment of a family member when they feel they need to slow their physician down but are afraid to ask or the internal conflict they experience if they risk disappointing their doctor by not going along with his or her recommendations. I have also witnessed loved ones endure difficult treatments with a low likelihood of success because they felt it was their role to do what the doctor said. Professionally, I am fortunate to work with a company whose mission is to be the catalyst for fundamentally changing how individuals are cared for during an advanced illness. Daily, I hear stories about the difficult choices that need to be made, and the effort it takes by patients to ensure their families and their health teams are hearing their voices. I continue to be energized by these stories and personal experiences, so I will continue to train and equip healthcare professionals with the tools and techniques needed to ease this burden and empower patients' voices.

10.9 Albert W. Wu MD, MPH

Bio

Albert W. Wu is practicing general internist and Professor of Health Policy and Management at the Johns Hopkins Bloomberg School of Public Health, with joint appointments in Epidemiology, International Health, Medicine and Surgery, and the Carey Business School. He directs the Center for Health Services and Outcomes Research, the PhD in Health

Services Research, and online Masters of Applied Science in Patient Safety & Healthcare Quality. He has been at Johns Hopkins since 1990, where his research and teaching focus on patient outcomes and quality of care. He developed widely used questionnaires to measure quality of life, adherence, satisfaction, attitudes, and behaviors for people with HIV and other chronic diseases. He was founder and director of the outcomes research committee of the AIDS Clinical Trials Group of the NIH, and President of the International Society for Quality of Life. He has been a thought leader in the integration of PROs into electronic health records, and their use for comparative effectiveness research, and leads PRO integration into EPIC for Johns Hopkins. He is co-principal investigator of a large CMMI-funded project to develop PRO performance measures for enhanced primary care (CPC+) practices nationwide. He has also studied patient safety since 1988. He was a member of the Institute of Medicine committee on identifying and preventing medication errors, Senior Adviser for Patient Safety to the World Health Organization (WHO) in Geneva, and is a member of the National Quality Forum Patient Safety Standing committee. He has authored over 400 peer-reviewed publications and is Editor-in-Chief of the Journal of Patient Safety and Risk Management. *He earned a BA and MD from Cornell University, and MPH from the University of California, Berkeley.*

How did you become interested in patient-reported outcomes?

At the very beginning of my career, I became involved in the first clinical trials of the first agents to treat what was then known as acquired immune deficiency syndrome (AIDS). One of the very first trials, at our center in San Diego, was a trial of azidothymidine (AZT). We enrolled 31 patients but when the trial was stopped prematurely after less than a year, there were 15 people still alive in the AZT group and three people alive in the placebo group. However, the people who are alive in the AZT group were not "healthy" by any means. They had symptoms that were caused by their disease and new symptoms from taking the medication. I became curious to know more about the impact of treatment not only on survival, but also on their functioning and how they felt. And so, I became interested in measuring this. I was fortunate to have access to researchers in Los Angeles at RAND and UCLA who were pioneers in measuring patient-reported outcomes, what they then called Health Related Quality of Life. John Ware was one of the primary people and Anita Stewart was another. There was another pioneering researcher, Bob Kaplan, at UC San Diego, who was interested in measuring quality of life and health utility. I was fortunate to work with these researchers examine the impact of treatment on patient quality of life, to develop short questionnaires that could be used in HIV clinical trials. One measure, the Medical Outcomes Study HIV Health Survey (MOS-HIV), has been used in more HIV trials than any other instrument. I led effort for the AIDS Clinical Trials Group of the NIH to systematically collect patient-reported outcome measures, and formed a scientific Outcomes Committee to accomplish this. As the work progressed, it became apparent that these measures could be relevant for other health states and other diseases, not just HIV.

I followed the clinical trials job with a research fellowship, and then went to work at Johns Hopkins, in part because of the work on patient-reported outcomes that I was doing. I was recruited to work with Marilyn Bergner, who was a third pioneer in measuring what she referred to as health status and who developed another leading measure, the Sickness Impact Profile. Looking back, I had incredibly good luck in getting to work with the people who truly built the foundation for measuring patient-reported outcome that my work built upon.

And are you using these in your daily work today?
I am. I continue to use them in research, and even to some extent in my own practice. And I'm charged with organizing

the systematic collection of patient-reported outcomes in our Epic electronic health record for Johns Hopkins Medicine.

What challenges have you come across as you tried to use them and tried to incorporate them more widely across Johns Hopkins?

There are a host of challenges that exist at every level of healthcare organizations. They include a lack of conviction that this is a worthwhile thing to do, or a lack of knowledge about what is involved to accomplish this work. In general, if you're not particularly well informed about what is involved, you imagine that it would be simpler, easier, and less expensive than it winds up being.

There are also many practical challenges. Most healthcare providers, physicians, and others don't believe or are not aware of how PROMs could be useful. They are unfamiliar with the specific tools, and even if they are familiar with a few, they don't know how to interpret them. They don't know what actions to take based on the information. This puts patient-reported outcome measures at a disadvantage relative to the conventional clinical measures, which are used in practice all the time. There are only a few existing health systems in the United States that collect the data systematically, routinely, and at scale. Most current clinical workflows in ambulatory care are not designed to do this. There are ways to collect PROs that are built into a few of the large electronic health records. But even in these cases, a rate-limiting step is the time and expense needed to program patient-reported outcome measures into that electronic health record.

In addition, patients—even though they believe in the concepts and would like doctors and others to know about what they're feeling and what they're experiencing—are also not aware of the usefulness of these tools. This is largely because they are also not familiar with them. They are not part of their general conception of medical practice. This is an additional challenge.

Finally, it is clear that everything isn't worked out in the field. To start out, in general, we do not yet know enough to be able to tell providers and patients precisely what the scores mean and what they should do with them.

If you were to speak about patient-reported outcomes to another organization or another set of providers, what advice would you give?

There are sociological challenges to address. These have to do with the culture of healthcare in every institution in general. There are traditions that dictate how care is delivered, and an existing evidence base that supports the use of certain tools, tests, and treatments. There is not yet a similar evidence base for patient-reported outcomes. It is not surprising that clinicians and managers are not yet trusting of them or they are suspicious, reluctant, or uncertain about what to do with them. If I were to advise an organization, it would be to work with someone who is in charge to build a set of shared knowledge and shared language. I would plan on what this would truly cost, as building the local knowledge and buy-in take time. If this education piece is done as an afterthought, things are unlikely to go well.

How do you see the future unfolding for the use of patient-reported outcomes?

I think that things are progressing, but exactly where it's going to go is uncertain. Like many things, it's evolving in fits and starts. Some enthusiasts have made quite a lot of progress. There are others who are lumbering along and suffering from the fact that they have not invested sufficient time, effort, or forethought into what strategies they should pursue in order to achieve those goals and vision.

In the meantime, there are competing developments, which are less systematic and but perhaps more consumer-centric at collecting various forms of patient-generated information. Currently, they are less scientifically based than validated patient-reported outcome measures. There is less of an evidence base for their value, but patient-reported measures are now beginning to compete with a variety of other kinds of patient-generated information, including information collected from phones and devices that can be used unobtrusively. In the future, these will become even more ubiquitous.

I think there is a natural selection process that is going on. And interestingly, it's not all within the professional sphere, but as everything is democratizing and information wants to be free, this new world is encroaching to some extent on what has previously been an expert domain.

Finally, I think that part of the vision is that data that reflects the patient's perspective could be collected and used for many things that could benefit both individual patients help improve decision-making, and could also add to the evidence base. In this way, the data could contribute to creating an agile, learning healthcare system. They might also potentially be used to help define what value is and help the system evolve towards providing greater value. Right now, the system is pretty heavily weighted towards what clinicians prefer and what they believe reflects the goals of healthcare. Because patients have more goals for their health and for their lives than simply healthcare, I think that there's a chance that wider incorporation of these measures into practice alongside conventional clinical measures could help us better achieve goals that truly matter to patients.

Summarizing the Interviews

As you likely know from your own healthcare experience and from the experiences of these subject matter experts, change is not always an easy proposition. It takes a "multilevel and multifocal" approach, as Dr. Rosengren said, to be successful.

There will be barriers. Some people in your organization might believe your care is already at the pinnacle of patient-centeredness and patient-focus (it likely isn't). Others might think this is all too complicated to implement (it does not have to be).

As with any change, the impetus for implementing these methods and processes must come from the top. As Dr. Bozic said:

> "You have to have buy-in from the leaders of the organization that this is a must-have, not a nice-to-have. So it begins by building shared language and shared knowledge among the organizational leadership and building commitment from the top that we will assess outcomes from the patient's perspective for every patient."

One message that comes through in these interviews is that if you make these changes, patients will see it. They will "get" the value to them in your approach, and this will likely be a refreshing experience for them compared to what they have known in the past at the point of care, and will empower them by "capturing their voice," as Ms. Hoy pointed out. And providers will see it in their own satisfaction. As Dr. Handley noted, "there is a joy that comes from making connections with patients."

I believe that particular joy goes both ways, and translates into a multitude of benefits for patients, providers, and their organizations—health-wise, career-wise, and business-wise.

10.10 Conclusion

When I set out to write this book and it was in its early stages, I jotted down many notes to be used for the pitch I might give to potential publishers in a query letter. How could I best and most concisely give them a sense of what drove me to write this and why I thought it would be important to healthcare provider organizations and people?

I told those prospective publishers I was writing "Finding What Matters Most for Patients" to give providers a better understanding of how to use patient-reported data to their advantage at the point of service and to give insight to patients about what this major shift in care means to them. I was going to provide the background for developing shared knowledge and shared language, along with extensive examples of dialogue between providers and patients using patient-reported outcome measures at several points in episodes of care. I was also planning to do personal interviews with subject matter experts who have significant experience using these measures.

My vision of the result? Readers would come away with a comprehensive understanding of this modern healthcare management opportunity, something nobody else was approaching quite in the way I did in this book. In the year I took to write this book, I believe I accomplished much of that. However, when you have worked through a project like this and conducted detailed interviews and collaborated with professionals who have made great strides in these areas, and spent countless hours bouncing ideas off colleagues, you eventually gain a deeper understanding of why you needed to do it.

My thinking on this has evolved. I believe the real reason I wrote this book was expressed wonderfully in Chapter 10 in my interview with Matt Handley, MD, of Kaiser Permanente of Washington. He seemed to sum up the true premise that got me started when he talked about the main challenges of taking the concepts and techniques detailed in this book and putting them into play across an entire enterprise:

> "The first is really the idea among care providers that, "I already do this." As clinicians, I think we judge ourselves by our intent, which is to provide person-centered care. I think that the vast majority of clinicians are working hard and doing their best based on how they were trained. This often includes the presumption that we already know a patient's

preferences. The evidence, however, demonstrates that our ability to implicitly grasp an individual patient's preferences and values is actually quite faulty. Our biggest barrier, then, is that we believe we are better at this than we are."

And that's the point. Fervently, this is what we want to do as clinicians and this is what we feel in our hearts we are doing when interacting with our patients. On our best days, this is true. We get tired. We get distracted. Our morals can be injured, scarring, and hardening our souls for a time. In these moments, we are not as good at communicating with our patients as we think we are. Good health outcomes are not all about healthcare. There is healing on both sides of the encounter when patients feel their experience at the point of care addressed the outcome that mattered most to them.

My hope is that this book helps you navigate toward what matters most—and find it.

Index

Printed in the United States
by Baker & Taylor Publisher Services